PEACE-MAKING AND
THE SETTLEMENT WITH JAPAN

BOOKS FROM
THE CENTER OF INTERNATIONAL STUDIES
Woodrow Wilson School of Public and International Affairs
Princeton University

Gabriel A. Almond, *The Appeals of Communism*
Gabriel A. Almond and James S. Coleman, editors, *The Politics of the Developing Areas*
Robert J. C. Butow, *Tojo and the Coming of the War*
Bernard C. Cohen, *The Political Process and Foreign Policy: The Making of the Japanese Peace Settlement*
Percy E. Corbett, *Law in Diplomacy*
Charles De Visscher, *Theory and Reality in Public International Law*, translated by P. E. Corbett
Frederick S. Dunn, *Peace-making and the Settlement with Japan*
Herman Kahn, *On Thermonuclear War*
W. W. Kaufmann, editor, *Military Policy and National Security*
Klaus Knorr, *The War Potential of Nations*
Klaus Knorr, editor, *NATO and American Security*
Klaus Knorr and Sidney Verba, editors, *The International System: Theoretical Essays*
Lucian W. Pye, *Guerrilla Communism in Malaya*
Rolf Sannwald and Jacques Stohler, *Economic Integration: Theoretical Assumptions and Consequences of European Unification*, translated by Herman F. Karreman
Glenn H. Snyder, *Deterrence and Defense*
Sidney Verba, *Small Groups and Political Behavior: A Study of Leadership*
Myron Weiner, *Party Politics in India*

PEACE-MAKING AND THE SETTLEMENT WITH JAPAN

BY FREDERICK S. DUNN

PRINCIPAL COLLABORATORS:
ANNEMARIE SHIMONY, PERCY E. CORBETT
BERNARD C. COHEN

PRINCETON, NEW JERSEY
PRINCETON UNIVERSITY PRESS
1963

Copyright © 1963
by Princeton University Press
All Rights Reserved
L.C. Card: 63-7155

Printed in the United States of America
by Princeton University Press,
Princeton, New Jersey

PREFACE

Professor Frederick S. Dunn died on March 17, 1962, before he could put the finishing touches on the manuscript of this book. He had been working on it for several years, at times assisted by Professors Corbett and Cohen and especially by Professor Annemarie Shimony who, in the middle 1950's, was a research assistant in the Center of International Studies. In pursuing his investigation of the subject, Professor Dunn had unusual access to State Department papers, many of which are classified and cannot be cited.

This book is not so much a full history of the stream of events, considerations, and actions in various parts of the world which influenced the peace made with Japan after the last war as an analytical case study of American decision-making—a case study which is unpretentious in method and extraordinarily rich in explanatory power.

It may indeed be said that, in writing this deeply reflective work, the author has drawn on all the insights gathered during his long and distinguished career. When associated with the Department of State as a legal officer in the 1920's, he observed both the extent to which actual decision-making differed from the formal procedures that were supposed to determine its course, and the extent to which the set of reasons given for particular decisions was at variance with the set that produced the result. He decided that he had to get outside the system in order to discover and apply the concepts that would give order to, and illuminate, the world he had observed from within. He then began his academic career, which led him to Johns Hopkins, Yale, and finally Princeton, and which made him in the 1930's and 1940's such a catalytic influence on American studies of international affairs.

During the 1920's and early 1930's, American scholars carried on important work in international law, diplomatic history, and international economics. With very few exceptions,

PREFACE

however, international *politics*—which, after all, goes to the heart of inter-state affairs—was grossly neglected as a field of systematic study, and the idea that international politics and foreign policy could be studied realistically only in terms of the behavior and characteristics of the actors was new and exciting. It was the application of this idea that Professor Dunn promoted both in his own writings and in the support he gave to the researches of many others. His initiative and example made the academic research organization an important instrument for work on international affairs, and by founding the quarterly *World Politics* in 1948 he gave the field a major medium for the circulation of research results.

In view of the enormous change in the American role in world affairs that took place during World War II and thereafter, Professor Dunn's work was of crucial importance to his country as well as to scholarship. Many of those now involved in developing this role learned much, directly or indirectly, from Professor Dunn, from his writing and teaching or, once removed, from those whose careers he guided and supported. Numerous passages in the present book testify to the intellectual qualities that made this process possible.

KLAUS KNORR

Center of International Studies
Princeton University, May 1, 1962

CONTENTS

Preface, by Klaus Knorr	v
Introduction	ix
I. Pre-Pearl Harbor Plans for Peace	3
II. Planning for Peace During Wartime	22
III. Peace-making and the Cold War	42
IV. Peace Proposals: 1947-1950	53
V. The Mission of John Foster Dulles	95
VI. Direct Negotiations on the Treaty	123
VII. The Economics of the Settlement	144
VIII. The San Francisco Conference of 1951	172
IX. Security in the Pacific	187
Index	205

INTRODUCTION

THE breadth and depth of the changes that have taken place in the international system since the close of World War II are starkly revealed in the course of events in the Far East following the surrender of Japan on the deck of the USS "Missouri" in 1945. The United States was at that time in a position of seemingly unassailable supremacy in the Pacific area. The Japanese had no recourse but to submit to whatever terms the victors chose to prescribe for the future control of the Pacific area. Save for the necessity of finding a basis of agreement among the Allied nations themselves, there seemed to be no substantial obstacle to the establishment of a secure and stable peace in that area.

After six years of intermittent sparring among the coalition members, a basis of agreement was finally found and a treaty of peace was signed by forty-eight nations and Japan in 1951. This treaty was and still is widely regarded as a notable diplomatic achievement. It was short, it was non-punitive, it restored sovereignty to the vanquished Japanese and sought to make them a willing partner in the free-world alliance.

Had the political world returned to the general pattern of the international system existing before the war, it seems possible that this treaty might have served as a useful and enduring basis for peace and security in the Pacific. But the world did not do so. Instead, it continued to move in the direction of profound revolutionary changes that brought about a realignment of the powers from a multiple balance-of-power system to a precarious bipolar division. This was accompanied by sweeping alterations in the status of colonial peoples everywhere as they moved toward independent statehood, as well as by explosive demographic changes that threatened serious pressures on the world's food resources. At the same time, there was taking place a terrifying revolution in the destructive

INTRODUCTION

power of military weapons which placed within range the possibility of demolishing whole centers of population.

The first thing to be noted, then, about the Japanese peace treaty is that it did not come into being at a quiet moment of impending peace, but was negotiated in a period of turbulence in the international arena during which new and conflicting forces of huge dimensions made their appearance. While it marked the end of the war between the Allies and Japan, it arrived in the midst of an onrushing struggle of global importance.

The second thing to be noted about the treaty is that it was predominantly an American achievement. The initiative and conception had been American; as such, it was an important declaration of American foreign policy in the Pacific and in Asia. It represented a divergence from prior policy that was almost revolutionary in character. The bloodiest of wars had ended with "the most Christian" of treaties; the bitter wartime enemy had suddenly become the peacetime ally; the traditional American solicitude for continental China had been replaced by an equal concern for insular Japan.

The shift in policy was not a sudden one but was a composite of countless tacks, compromises, and reappraisals in a rapidly changing world. As in all major policy alterations, the new policy was not the result of a single deliberate decision but of much probing and groping by many people. Those steering the new course had to contend with the customary obstacles of intellectual inertia, precedent, conformity, bureaucracy, and the lagging pace of public opinion. These very human contingencies go far to explain actions which, ten years later, may appear obvious, pedestrian, or outdated. A bold conception a decade ago may seem a *sine qua non* today; a difficult decision then may seem to us only an obvious logical consequence.

No peace treaty is constructed *in vacuo*. It proceeds directly from the conflict it aims to settle and presumably addresses

INTRODUCTION

itself to a restoration of international order in a particular environment. Unfortunately, international order is a concept not always isolated by statesmen or other policy-molders from the national interests of their respective countries; thus the restoration of "normal" conditions by an erstwhile war coalition is at best a complicated and difficult process. When the wartime alliance breaks up into separate competing national units, many problems other than the restitution of sovereignty to the vanquished and the establishment of war guilt enter into the negotiations of a general peace. This is what happened in the case of the Japanese settlement.

The evolution of American policies regarding the Japanese peace settlement falls conveniently into four periods. The first runs from the outbreak of the war to the final defeat of Japan in 1945 and the dissolution of the wartime coalition into Communist and non-Communist camps. Under the pressure of events, both the policy planners of the United States and the public at large during this period changed drastically their assumptions about the probable course of our foreign affairs in the future. The discussion of this period in Chapters I and II has two primary aims: the first is to summarize the metamorphosis of national thinking from predominant isolationism and idealism to predominant internationalism and a greater emphasis on *Realpolitik*. The second is to examine the extent to which commitments and decisions (as well as the absence of them) originating in a discarded mode of thought remained to bedevil later policy designers. The results of past thinking—in the form of wartime agreements at Potsdam and Yalta, anti-Axis sentiments generated during the war, and the commitments in China—presented obstacles to rational planning regarding the Far East, and particularly Japan.

The second section deals with the years 1945-1950 and comprises Chapters III and IV. During this period the existence of the Cold War was generally acknowledged by those

INTRODUCTION

who formed the policies of the United States, and it was recognized that planning for the peace in any specific area should be subsumed under general plans to assure the security of the United States against the Soviet Union. During this period, however, many different perspectives on national security led to conflicting strategies and tactics being proposed. The central question considered in this section is how a general policy toward Japan, with a definite agenda for a peace treaty, began to crystallize from the points of view of various agencies and individuals.

The third section, Chapters V-VIII, concerns the events of the years 1950 and 1951. During this time John Foster Dulles conducted intensive negotiations that culminated in the conference in San Francisco, where forty-eight nations signed the treaty of peace with Japan. Despite the incorporation into the treaty of various suggestions made by Japan and our allies, it was clearly an American document. The main question to be investigated in this section is what Mr. Dulles' policies and tactics were for working toward the overt aims of the United States.

The fourth and final section considers the effect of the settlement on the security of the Western powers in the years since the treaty went into effect. In assessing the practical working out of the settlement, we have endeavored to keep in mind that "20-20 hindsight" is not really fair to men who had to plan without the benefit of augury.

Peace-making, like war-making, is a series of decisions made by identifiable human beings acting in various capacities—as individuals, as national officials, as conference delegates, as party members, and so forth. By scrutinizing these decisions and the routes by which they were reached we may be able to acquire useful information for future peace-making. But decision-making in public affairs is a very complex operation and is hampered by many obstacles.

INTRODUCTION

Thus the makers of foreign policy are caught up in an archaic vocabulary which compels them to talk as if their respective nations made all the decisions and they themselves had little or nothing to do with them. At many times, of course, this is a convenient form of compression, but it often conceals and distorts the real political process which goes on behind the curtain of official anonymity. It also encourages the continuation of such persistent mysticisms as the organism theory of the state, which endows this mental construction with an existence and a will of its own, and sometimes even with arms and legs and a soul. One can escape from these fantasies only by looking directly at the decision-making activities which comprise the political process. This sounds simple enough but is in fact very difficult, because old intellectual habits persist in getting in the way.

In analyzing a policy-making operation it is not sufficient to accept the final decisions and explanations publicly offered by the decision-maker. It is necessary to go back to the original doubts or dilemmas as they were presented to him, and to observe the ways he approached them and the devices he employed to solve or evade them. The specific difficulties to which the perplexities of responsible policy-makers can be traced fall generally into four classes: (1) dilemmas of competing values, aims, or principles; (2) incomplete or imperfect information; (3) uncertainties of prediction; and (4) the difficulties of reaching accord with others sharing the decision-making power.

Most political action can be summed up as the business of encountering, grappling with, and resolving or evading a series of more or less difficult dilemmas. A dilemma, as the term is here used, is a doubt that cannot readily be resolved by simple logic or the discovery of some fact. Almost always a dilemma involves, explicitly or implicitly, a hard choice between principles or values. It is seldom a case of choice between good and bad, or right and wrong, but between things that are partly

INTRODUCTION

desirable and partly undesirable, and there is no easy way of weighing the relative advantages. The difficulty, in other words, lies not in failing to find an applicable principle but in finding too many of them, each leading to a different answer. The decision between them invariably requires the sacrifice of some values for others, and seldom pleases everybody.

If people generally understood that this type of perplexity is the normal daily fare of statesmen, they would perhaps be more charitable in their judgments about them. By whatever instrumentality a decision-maker chooses to resolve his dilemmas, there is always a price to be paid and it is difficult to know in advance whether the result is worth it. Since the available principles by themselves cannot solve the dilemma, he is generally compelled to project his thinking forward to the possible consequences of following different courses of action and to try to decide which is the more desirable. But this involves an inescapable risk that things will not turn out as he expected. Yet he will be charged with the consequences of his choice, as if he knew with certainty what would happen and hence must have desired what really happened. On the other hand, he may make a choice blindly and without reason and it may turn out in the end to work very favorably for his country. In such a case it is not unusual for him to claim full credit for the foresight which he did not really have.[1]

The second type of perplexity—that arising from incomplete or imperfect information about a particular situation—needs little discussion. Policy-makers are generally backstopped by groups of busy fact-finders whose duty is to cope with this hazard. Often the incompleteness of the information is due to

[1] Harold Nicolson once described this process as follows: "At some international conference, for instance, a statesman achieves a given result which in the end proves of the utmost advantage to his country. In his subsequent memoirs he will almost surely disclose a greater degree of prevision, a more definite consciousness of motive, than he was himself aware of at the time, thereby establishing a logical (and personally creditable) sequence of cause and effect." ("Men and Circumstance," *Foreign Affairs*, XXIII, No. 3 [April 1945], p. 476.)

INTRODUCTION

the fact that a conflict exists and some relevant facts are concealed by the opponent. The intelligence machinery of the government is designed to overcome this obstacle as far as possible.

While incompleteness of factual information is the popular explanation for the difficulties of statesmanship, a case could be made for saying that it is less often the cause for the grey hairs of policy-makers than the persistence of dilemmas, as described above. If it is only a missing fact that is the cause of a doubt, there are few limits to the ingenuity of pursuers of information. Even where the elusive fact relates to an undisclosed intention in the mind of an opponent, there are techniques available for narrowing down the possibilities so closely that the importance of the doubt is minimized.

Often what is regarded as a question of fact is really a dilemma of principle. Decision-makers are always hoping that they will discover some piece of factual information that will save them from the necessity of making difficult choices.

The third type of perplexity—that arising from unavoidable uncertainties in prediction—is also too familiar to need much discussion. Where human behavior is involved, the risks of forecasting are always formidable.

Yet here too a considerable amount of progress has been made in improving the techniques for estimating probabilities. Officials and others can and do act all day long on the basis of their expectations as to the future conduct of other people. It is still true that, within certain realms of action, men act rationally a good portion of the time and can be counted upon to do so. Where their behavior is affected by other influences, such as cultural predispositions or fixed attitudes acquired from association with particular groups, the problems of forecasting are more complex but no longer have to be solved blindly or without evidence.

Even the aims of the most rational decision-makers are frequently thwarted by the unforeseen effects of their decisions.

INTRODUCTION

Within a particular set of circumstances a choice of action may seem quite reasonable, but it starts a chain of consequences outside the calculations of the decision-maker. Thus an unintended effect of our decision to withdraw our troops from Korea in 1948 was to create the impression that a future aggression there would not be resisted by the United States. The original decision was based on strategic considerations which were probably sound, but the unintended effects counteracted its value. Careful planning may reduce the dangers from unintended effects of decisions, but there is no present hope of being able to eliminate them altogether.

In the international field, the problems of building up good expectations on which to make decisions is of course greatly complicated by the fact that people in different cultures must be expected to have different responses to given situations. Our knowledge of the ways in which cultural attitudes affect human behavior and also what can be done to modify such attitudes is still in an early stage, but it is growing rapidly. At the same time, the obvious fact that these differences arising out of different cultures exist is a constant warning to policy-makers not to assume that, because they think in a certain way, other people will think in the same way. At any rate, there is no longer much excuse for decision-makers to pick their expectations about human behavior out of the thin air of idle speculation. There is plenty of knowledge now available to correct the folklore that used to fill up the medicine bags of the old practitioners of diplomacy.

The fourth and perhaps most exasperating type of perplexity arises out of the division of the decision-making power among many people and the resulting need for a policy-maker constantly to bring about some accord between his own views and those of others. In international decisions there is of course not merely the problem of the sharing of the decision-making power with various agencies and people within the country, but also that of persuading people in other countries

INTRODUCTION

to go along with the decision. There is the further complication that in the international arena no final resting place of the decision-making power exists and hence there is no appeal to recognized authority in the absence of voluntary accord.

To get all of the accord necessary for achieving effective action, the policy-maker often has to make various compromises with different forms of opposition, until what he ends up with may bear little resemblance to what he started out to attain. This seems to be an inescapable part of the democratic process, and there is no suggestion that it is intrinsically wrong. Nevertheless, it is one of the principal causes of perplexity for policy-makers and exercises an obvious influence on the formulation of policies.

Of course the decision-maker has many ways of persuading those who share the decision-making power to go along with him. Rational argument is one of them, but he soon learns that it is of limited power in the presence of fixed attitudes and rigid conceptions of interest. How to communicate with people in order to modify or get around these rooted points of view has received considerable attention of late. As a subject of inquiry it has produced many good insights, but it is also full of danger, since men of evil intention can use its devices as well as responsible decision-makers.

In the case of the Japanese settlement, the difficulties of policy-planning were immensely increased by the fact that it was a coalition peace and a large number of nations had to be brought into the negotiations. Coalition peace-making is at best a highly difficult business. The noticeable unity that binds together the members of an alliance when faced with a common enemy is apt to disappear into thin air when the pressure is lifted. Then the diversities of interest among the allies come to the surface and harass the peace-makers. The hatreds engendered by the war and the losses sustained by the individual members of the coalition tend to produce a far greater ac-

INTRODUCTION

cumulation of demands on the defeated enemy than could ever be satisfied.

Finally, there are the obstacles to policy-planning arising from stupidity, ignorance, intolerance, and plain inertia on the part of those with whom statesmen have to deal. While less dangerous, perhaps, than the hazards thrown up by evil men, they are more exasperating because there is generally very little that can be done about them in meeting an immediate situation. It has long been known that patience is a prime requirement for successful statesmanship.

Taken as a whole, and considering all the perplexities involved, the public view of the conception and execution of the Japanese peace settlement as a first-class example of coalition peace-making seems justified. In a sharply divided world the negotiators achieved a high degree of unity in restoring Japan to a respected place in the international system and keeping her aligned with the Western powers. After a decade of operation the peace treaty is still the guidepost for Japan's role in the postwar world.

In the following pages we shall look at this unique enterprise with a view to seeing what wisdom can be distilled out of it. One obvious conclusion is that, in order to understand the significance of the settlement, it is necessary to see it in terms of our foreign relations as a whole and not merely of our policy toward Japan. It is also necessary to observe it from the beginning of our hostile relations with Japan, rather than to confine ourselves to the specific negotiations undertaken by Mr. Dulles. Thirdly, it is essential to approach the settlement as a sequence of concrete choices of action in problematic situations by identifiable individuals rather than by abstract political institutions.

PEACE-MAKING AND
THE SETTLEMENT WITH JAPAN

CHAPTER I

PRE-PEARL HARBOR PLANS FOR PEACE

PLANNING a foreign policy for the postwar world started very soon after the outbreak of World War II in Europe in 1939 and before the United States had become a participant. At that time President Roosevelt and the State Department were waging a campaign against isolationism and were determined that the United States should have an important role in the formulation of any postwar settlement. Thus President Roosevelt in his Neutrality Address of September 3, 1939, insisted that "when peace has been broken anywhere, peace of all countries everywhere is in danger," and added that "the influence of America should be consistent in seeking for humanity a final peace which will eliminate, as far as it is possible to do so, the continued use of force between nations."[1] At the same time Secretary of State Hull declared that it was essential in America's "own best interest" to throw "the weight of our country's moral and material influence in the direction of creating a stable and enduring order under law."[2]

The first specific planning assignment in the State Department to deal with postwar problems (September 16, 1939) was given to Leo Pasvolsky, a native Russian who had come to the United States at an early age and had become an economist serving with the Brookings Institution and with the State Department. Soon afterward a committee, later known as the Advisory Committee on Problems of Foreign Relations, was established to "survey the basic principles which should underlie a desirable world order to be evolved after the termi-

---

[1] *Department of State Bulletin* (hereafter cited as DSB), I, No. 11 (September 9, 1939), pp. 201-2.
[2] Quoted in Ruth B. Russell, *A History of the United Nations Charter: The Role of the United States, 1940-1945*, Washington, D.C., Brookings Institution, 1958, p. 17.

nation of present hostilities, with primary reference to the best interests of the United States."[3] Under Secretary of State Welles was named chairman of this Committee and among the members were a number of senior officers of the State Department. There were three subcommittees, one political, one economic (under the chairmanship of Pasvolsky), and one concerned with the limitation and reduction of armaments. An unpublished directive to the Committee was "to study means whereby the war might be limited and possibly ended, the foundations of a peaceful world order laid, and the defense of the Western Hemisphere strengthened."[4]

Because of the urgency of immediate international problems, the meetings of the Committee were sporadic and it eventually became little more than an instrument of current policy. However, several proposals of a longer-range nature were formulated, and these are interesting as indicating the patterns of thinking on international matters that were prevailing at the time. The political subcommittee considered the implications of a possible German victory and recommended the revision of the neutrality legislation then in force in the United States. The economic subcommittee produced an outline concerning postwar economic relations and postwar limitations of armaments. This was to be submitted to a projected conference of neutrals to consider, among other things, "the most effective means, upon the conclusion of the war, of securing a stable world order based upon international law and a sound international economic system."[5] It was thought that the neutral nations, including the United States, could form a bloc which would have more influence than any of them could have singly, and that this bloc would be linked by

[3] [Harley Notter], *Postwar Foreign Policy Preparation, 1939-1945* (hereafter cited as PWFPP), Department of State Publication 3580, General Foreign Policy Series 15, Washington, D.C., G.P.O., 1949, p. 20.
[4] *The Memoirs of Cordell Hull* (hereafter cited as *Memoirs*), 2 vols., New York, Macmillan, 1948, pp. 732, 1627; Russell, *op.cit.*, pp. 17ff.
[5] Under Secretary of State Welles, quoted in Russell, *op.cit.*, p. 18.

"commitments with respect to the basic principles of sound and stable international relationships after the war."[6] But official thinking about sound international order was focused primarily on the European and American scene and did not extend to the Far East.

The proposed conference of neutrals was never held because the German invasion of Norway ended the "phony war." Germany's successes in the spring of 1940 led State Department officials to think that postwar planning must take into account the very real possibility of a German victory. The agency for this new line of planning was the Interdepartmental Group to Consider Postwar International Economic Problems and Policies. The nucleus of this organ was the economic subcommittee of the Advisory Committee, plus members from the Departments of the Treasury, Commerce, and Agriculture.

In October 1940 the Group held a series of meetings devoted to postwar problems. A type of planning was sought which could be used as a basis for action regardless of the outcome of the war. It was decided that this requirement could best be fulfilled by a comprehensive survey of the international commodity market, which would in turn illuminate the underlying economic structure of regional blocs and would lead to an appraisal of the economic capacities of various countries and regions. Eight subgroups dealing with specific commodities and four subgroups dealing with regions were established, with Pasvolsky endeavoring to coordinate the research findings. But because of the regular departmental tasks of the members, the activities of the Group diminished, and by March 1941 it had ceased to meet. A Division of Special Research had been formed in February 1941, and it carried on at intervals some of the detailed work of fact-finding and reporting on economic matters initiated by the Interdepartmental Group.[7]

[6] PWFPP, p. 25.
[7] *Ibid.*, p. 43. The Division of Special Research had been conceived

PRE-PEARL HARBOR PLANS FOR PEACE

The establishment of the above agencies did not, of course, mean that all State Department consideration of postwar problems was localized in them. Various individual policy-planners were thinking independently about postwar matters, and some of their opinions eventually became the consensus of the Department. For example, as early as the fall of 1941 it was felt that a monolithic peace conference, after the pattern of Versailles, would be a mistake, and that it would also be a mistake to make the establishment of any postwar version of the League of Nations a part of the peace treaty. It was proposed instead that the settlement should take place in three stages: a transition from war to peace prior to the making of peace arrangements; the conclusion of such arrangements; and a period in which they would become effective. It was also assumed at this time that the USSR would participate in postwar decisions.

The goals and values that guided the postwar planning of the State Department at the time were reflected in public declarations of Secretary Hull and President Roosevelt. Thus Hull, in a radio address on May 18, 1941, stated that the Department was at work on the task of creating ultimate conditions of peace with justice, and that consideration was being given to the following principles necessary to this task: extreme nationalism must be restrained from ever again imposing excessive trade restrictions; international commercial relations must be the rule; raw materials should be available to all; supplies of commodities must be handled in the interest of consuming countries; international finance should aid the development of all countries and permit reasonable methods

---

by Pasvolsky as a separate agency to deal with the collection and analysis of basic facts, and to serve as a secretariat for the Interdepartmental Group, on the theory that the division of labor between research and policy-making would promote efficiency. This conception was not fulfilled because of the lapsing of the Interdepartmental Group, although later, when the Advisory Committee on Postwar Foreign Policy was formed in December 1941, the Division of Special Research did serve as a kind of secretariat for it. See below.

of payment. Hull warned that unless such a system became firmly established, international instability would be chronic.[8]

In the same lofty vein Secretary Hull, in reply to a Congressional inquiry about American peace plans, informed the Senate Committee on Foreign Relations that the Department of State was concerned with "defining and formulating the broad objectives of desirable post-war policies, comprising the restoration of order under law in international relations; the elimination of the crushing burden of competitive armaments; and the creation of the kind of international commercial and financial relations which are essential to the preservation of stable peace and to the promotion of economic welfare for the peoples of all nations."[9]

By far the most important statement of postwar objectives was the Atlantic Charter issued by President Roosevelt and Prime Minister Churchill in the summer of 1941. In contrast to the cloudy aspirations expressed in the Hull declarations, the eight points of the Charter provided reasonably clear, although not necessarily attainable, targets. They were briefly as follows:

No territorial aggrandizement.
No territorial changes which did not accord with the freely expressed wishes of the peoples concerned.
The right of peoples to choose the form of government under which they would live and a restoration of government and sovereign rights to those now forcibly deprived of them.
Equal access (with due respect for existing obligations) to trade and to raw materials needed for economic prosperity.
Economic collaboration among nations for the sake of improved labor standards, economic advancement, and social security.
Freedom from want and fear.
Freedom of the seas.
Reduction of armaments and abandonment of force pending the establishment of a wider and permanent system of general security.

[8] DSB, IV, No. 99 (May 17, 1941), pp. 573-77.
[9] PWFPP, p. 47.

PRE-PEARL HARBOR PLANS FOR PEACE

It will be recalled that, when this joint declaration was issued on August 11, 1941, the United States was still not at war and Pearl Harbor was nearly five months in the future. Nevertheless, it continued to serve thereafter as a blueprint of American postwar aims, and it was thought to be a common basis to which all the anti-Axis powers could subscribe.

This assumption had important consequences. Throughout the war years it enabled the State Department to oppose definite commitments prior to the peace settlements on the ground that the Atlantic Charter sufficed for interim understanding, while any secret treaties or commitments could lead to the same sort of confusion as at Versailles. Even before Pearl Harbor, Hull had instructed the United States Ambassador in London to warn Eden against secret commitments in his dealings with Stalin. Such commitments on specific terms of postwar settlements could not but interfere with our earnest desire to aid Great Britain and the Soviet Union. Since the Atlantic Charter provided a common ground for postwar arrangements, it was proper to hold discussions which would further agreement on basic policies and prepare for future consensus; but specific terms must be settled after the war by all the nations which contributed to the victory.[10]

In September 1941, the Soviet Union, together with other states, formally adhered to the terms of the Atlantic Charter. However, the Soviet Ambassador to London made a subsequent qualification which was more significant than it seemed at the time: "Considering that the practical application of these principles *will necessarily adapt itself to the circumstances, needs, and historic peculiarities of particular countries*, the Soviet Government can state that a consistent application of these principles will secure the most energetic

---

[10] *Memoirs*, pp. 1165-66. See also William L. Langer and S. Everett Gleason, *The Undeclared War, 1940-1941*, New York, Harper, 1953, p. 825.

support on the part of the government and peoples of the Soviet Union."[11]

When Eden went to Moscow in December 1941, he was informed by Stalin of the Soviet government's conception of what the peace should be like. This included detailed proposals regarding territorial settlements in Europe, for which Stalin desired immediate British recognition. However, Hull's view prevailed and the British insisted that boundary questions could be settled only after the war.

Assumptions Underlying the Planning for Peace

Underlying the above proclamations and declarations were a number of familiar assumptions and ideas about the nature of the international system. To a large extent, they were premises operating in the thought of Secretary Hull. However, this is not so important as the fact that they constituted an intellectual tradition that was suffused throughout the State Department and other agencies of government.

A primary assumption was the interdependence of nations. In part this was simply a familiar deduction from historical experience—the growing trade relations among nations, the fact that wars among the great powers tended to engulf other nations against their will, and the manner in which economic depressions in one region tended to have repercussions in other regions. In part, however, this assumption had been elevated into a doctrine by Woodrow Wilson and others of an idealist bent who sought to institutionalize the interdependence of nations. In either its Wilsonian or its simple pragmatic form, it ran counter to the strong sentiment of isolationism then held by large sections of the American people.

A second assumption was that the relations among nations were regulated by a body of universal principles of law and

[11] Quoted in Russell, *op.cit.*, p. 44; italics added by Miss Russell.

morality, and that the habit of recourse to such principles would be revived and strengthened after the war.

Apparently Mr. Hull's expectations along this line were influenced more by his belief in the importance of a rule of law among nations than by any realistic appraisal of the probable behavior of governments in the postwar period. It is well known that, after coalition wars, coalitions tend to splinter into more or less antagonistic parts, and this is not a healthy climate for the growth of the rule of law. As a general rule, the revival of the legal habit comes *after* the restoration of order and stability and not before it, and the larger the war, the longer the period that is required for such restoration.

What was even more important, the Communist program was a revolutionary challenge to the traditional concept of the nature of the international system, and the Communists could hardly be expected to return voluntarily to the regulatory norms of the system they were attacking. In fact, they declined to accept any arrangements whereby their decisions on controversies could be overruled by an impartial agency—the minimum condition on which a workable legal system can endure.

A third and closely related assumption was that lawful and moral behavior of nations is not only good in the abstract but a matter of self-interest; in other words, what benefits the community of nations will also benefit each one singly. E. H. Carr calls this the "harmony of interests."[12] It is of course not entirely the product of wishful thinking. In the ordinary course of relations it is generally to the advantage of most nations to have things carried on in accordance with fixed rules. The possibility of retaliation for failure to comply with particular usages is generally enough to reveal the mutual advantage of regular procedures. In a nuclear age,

[12] Carr analyzes this thesis in *The Twenty Years' Crisis, 1919-1939*, London, Macmillan, 1940, pp. 54-80 and *passim*.

PRE-PEARL HARBOR PLANS FOR PEACE

it needs little argument to support the position that the avoidance of major wars is to the interest of each nation as well as to the advantage of the community at large.

On the other hand, in a world of limited resources, growing population pressures, nationalistic urges, and long-standing feelings of insecurity, there are many situations in which a gain for one nation is a loss for another. This is very generally true of territorial claims and competing demands for fishing rights and the like. In these cases it is hard to convince the nations lacking in resources that what is good for the international society is necessarily good for them. The assumption of the "harmony of interests" naturally appeals most strongly to the "have" nations—those which are more or less content with the *status quo*. Those which for real or imaginary reasons consider themselves to be among the "have-not" nations are likely to look upon assertions of the mutual advantages of maintenance of the *status quo* as mere hypocrisy.

Unhappily for the assumption of the "harmony of interests" of nations, there is no way of effecting changes in the existing distribution of territory, resources, and people except by the voluntary acquiescence of the parties or by war. Hence, unless the *status quo* is to be frozen permanently, there is little reason to assume that dissatisfied states will be pacified by appeals to the effect that the interest of the whole society of nations is the interest of each.

In the postwar planning, the American proposals both for limitations on armaments and for the removal of excessive trade restrictions assumed the acceptance of a substantial degree of harmony of interests. It appears that the optimism concerning postwar cooperation of the wartime coalition was explicitly based upon the belief by American officials that the United States, Great Britain, the Soviet Union, and China had no basic conflicts of interest. This proved to be quite wrong.

The above premises were instrumental in shaping official thinking on postwar planning in two important directions—one of them related to the role of force in international relations, and the other to economic cooperation among nations.

The premise regarding the legal and moral nature of the international system tended to play down the role of force and the maintenance in readiness of large-scale military power in peacetime. The rule of law presumably left little room for the resort to force, except in collective action against possible aggressors; and moral condemnation by the community of nations was regarded as a potent deterrent against violations of the peace. Furthermore, the premise of harmony of interests was thought to be incompatible with the use of force, since the latter endangered the community at large and hence each member of it. In the postwar planning prior to the Pearl Harbor attack, there was not much provision for instruments of force and there was frequent condemnation of power politics. Little was said about any need for maintaining a balance of power. In fact, the prevailing sentiment on the use of force was not very different from the isolationist view, although the premises were quite different.

Under the secretaryship of Hull, who as a senator had done important work in tariff reduction and international monetary agreements, the official view of the State Department looked upon economic cooperation as a major instrument in conducting foreign relations. The interdependence of nations was considered to be due primarily to the fact that none was economically self-sufficient, and that trade benefited all since nations with different resources could complement each other. Such an economic version is apparent in Hull's statement of the conditions of peace and justice, mentioned above, in which he maintained that extreme nationalism must not be allowed ever again to express itself in excessive trade restrictions.[18]

[18] See above, p. 7.

PRE-PEARL HARBOR PLANS FOR PEACE

The United States Becomes a Belligerent

Up to the present time we have been discussing the attitudes and plans of American officials in regard to the future peace settlement before the United States had even been drawn into the war. From this position on the sidelines the United States enjoyed a certain freedom in telling the belligerents what kind of a world system they should set up when the fighting was over.

After Pearl Harbor, the attention of our leaders shifted more to the business of winning the war itself. President Roosevelt certainly gave this priority in his thinking. The Declaration by United Nations, which he signed on January 1, 1942, stated that each Allied government would employ its full resources in the war and none of them would enter into a separate armistice or peace. The only reference to the future terms of peace was an acknowledgment in the Preamble of the existence of "a common program of purposes and principles embodied in the . . . Atlantic Charter."

There seemed to be little notion that any connection existed between the specific peace aims of the belligerents and the way in which the war was fought. Thus Secretary Hull insisted on his position that any political and territorial commitments during the war concerning the postwar world would not only inhibit the Allies from pressing the war to an unquestionable conclusion, but would also endanger a lasting peace, even as did the secret treaties after World War I. He reiterated his tenet of "no wartime specific commitments" at every opportunity. At the making of the Declaration by United Nations, he expressed his feeling that "the Allies should all be committed in advance to certain principles, leaving details of boundary adjustments and the like to be settled later. If the principles were strongly enough proclaimed and adhered to, the details would find readier solution when the time came to solve them."[14] This attitude would

[14] *Memoirs*, p. 1116.

seem to have precluded any negotiated peace settlement based on specific terms stated in advance of the termination of hostilities. Only a total victory by one side could provide the necessary authority for applying the general principles to specific situations.

In general the President, who conceived of himself primarily as Commander-in-Chief, was not actively concerned with postwar matters. He kept his own counsel with the Joint Chiefs of Staff and his personal advisers, and he took a rather cavalier attitude toward the operations of the State Department, not discouraging its future planning, but on the whole not giving it much attention.[15]

Unfortunately the personality and *modus operandi* of the Secretary of State contributed to the relegation of the State Department to a peripheral status. Hull was principally concerned with elevated principles, notably the adherence to law and morality in international dealings and freedom of trade among nations. Ironically, however, the means by which he attempted to achieve his sweeping ideals involved minute and undeviating adherence to legal obligations and detailed fact-finding investigations. Roosevelt, on the other hand, was impatient of formalities, legalities, and details. Furthermore, Hull tended to be extremely cautious, both in his desire to consider all possible alternatives before arriving at a decision, and in his solicitude for Congressional approval, whereas Roosevelt was temperamentally much bolder. It is true that the President approved of Hull's unwillingness to make territorial or other commitments prior to the peace conference; but Hull's obduracy on this point was a matter of conviction, whereas Roosevelt's concurrence was probably more attributable to his concentration upon the war itself.

Although the State Department was opposed to any plan-

---

[15] Cf. Herbert Feis, *The China Tangle: The American Effort in China from Pearl Harbor to the Marshall Mission*, Princeton, N.J., Princeton University Press, 1953, pp. 61, 103, and 106.

ning which verged upon advance commitments, it nevertheless claimed primary responsibility for general postwar policies. Hull viewed with suspicion the delegation of postwar policy-making to any newly established agency, particularly to Henry Wallace's Economic Defense Board (later called the Board of Economic Warfare). Consequently, on December 22, 1941, Hull proposed—and the President approved—a special committee in the State Department, the Advisory Committee on Postwar Foreign Policy, which was to evolve a postwar program in the interrelated fields of general security, limitation of armaments, sound international economic relationships, and other phases of international cooperation, the implementation of which was considered essential to enduring world peace and economic progress.[16] The Committee was to consist not only of State Department personnel, but of representatives from other government agencies, some Congressmen, and some private individuals of policy-planning competence. The results would be a judicious composite of various points of view.

At the first meeting of the Committee, Welles explained that "by direction of the President, only this Committee and, in a more limited field, the group of officials gathered under Vice President Wallace as Chairman of the Board of Economic Warfare were making authorized preparations concerning postwar foreign policy, and the recommendations of both were to be channeled to the President through the Secretary of State. The President desired to be able to reach in his basket and find there whatever he needed in regard to postwar foreign policy and meanwhile wished to devote himself wholly to ways and means of winning the war. It was

[16] Hull was already convinced that, in order to avoid the mistakes made in the peace settlement following World War I, he must gain the commitment of the political parties to any future plan, particularly to an international organization in which the United States would have a leading role. He therefore strove "to make the membership absolutely nonpartisan, and to give Republicans as well as Democrats adequate representation." (*Memoirs*, p. 1635.)

left to the Committee itself to determine the problems ahead and to provide the information and recommendations needed in dealing with those problems."[17]

A few weeks later Hull further defined the domain of the Committee as being strictly that of postwar problems; current decisions and policy were to be simply assumed as "given." It still did not seem to be adequately recognized that the decisions which the military departments and the President would inevitably make during wartime would have some influence on the postwar configurations. According to this view, the war was a crusade against evil men, and these had to be exterminated before a peace settlement could be designed. Whether the peacetime gains to be derived from the extra effort necessary to obtain unconditional surrender were worth it received surprisingly little public discussion in the United States. They may well have been, but it is hardly a question that could be decided rationally offhand.

The Advisory Committee on Postwar Foreign Policy met as a whole only until May 1942, but its various subcommittees—on economic policy, economic reconstruction, political problems, security problems, and territorial problems—continued their meetings until July 1943, and it was in these bodies that the most detailed postwar planning took place. The Division of Special Research, which had been established prior to Pearl Harbor,[18] served as a secretariat and research organization for the Advisory Committee and its subcommittees.

Several principles guided the deliberations of these groups. In the first place, it was considered more important to work out an overall program of desirable international principles than to fix upon a minimum of essential postwar policies. The primary objective was to be international security based upon justice, and problems were to be looked at from the point of view of this ideal, although of course with practical inter-

[17] PWFPP, pp. 78-79.   [18] See above, p. 5.

national considerations always kept in mind. But the common conception of security was protection against the then existing enemies and was based on the ideals of disarmament and collective security. Apparently none of the planners, including Secretary Hull, had a glimmering of what the real pattern of the international system would look like in the decades immediately following the war.

A second principle of procedure was that speed and decisive action were to be subordinated to the weighing of all possible alternatives. Because events were changing the world picture so rapidly and because American responsibility in maintaining an international settlement was such a radical change in our historic position, it was thought unwise to hurry into the new situation. Even after all alternatives were surveyed, final decisions were to be left in abeyance until the end of the war. Clearly Hull's cautious temperament was in part responsible for this procedural principle.

Finally, as a corollary to the insistence upon mature deliberation, it was deemed necessary to conduct careful studies of the factual background of all the possible alternatives. Consequently, reports were drawn up on a myriad of subjects relating to population, economic resources, historical associations, internal forces in various regions, and so forth. These studies were similar to those produced in the House Inquiry, which was established during World War I outside the State Department. It is interesting to note that the studies of the Inquiry were in large part responsible for the detailed knowledge of the world situation which the American delegation displayed at Versailles—as well, perhaps, as for its orientation toward an idealistic settlement.[19]

In March 1942, the Advisory Committee as a whole adopted a recommendation of the Subcommittee on Political Problems that peace should be restored in stages, an idea which

[19] Harold Nicolson, *Peacemaking, 1919*, New York, Harcourt, Brace, 1939, pp. 27-28.

had originated earlier in the State Department.[20] The Subcommittee recommended that during the initial armistice period, not to exceed a year, the immediate disturbances created by the war would be rectified: relief and rehabilitation of devastated regions would be initiated, provisional governments would be organized in enemy and liberated territories, codes of justice (incorporating the idea of war criminals) would be established in order to judge complaints against enemy oppressors, and agreement would be reached on the powers and authority to be vested in an organization of the United Nations.

During the transition period, which was to be of indefinite length, the individual enemy states and their governmental structures would be reconstituted with such political, economic, and regional groupings as the major powers determined, while these powers maintained such authority as would further the restoration of normal life in the enemy areas. It would be during this period that boundaries, population settlements, restitutions and reparations, and the *modus operandi* of various international economic institutions would be determined. Thereafter, the era of permanent peace would be inaugurated, in which there would be a strong international organization capable of keeping the *status quo* as established in the transition period.[21]

In sum, the postwar world was to be cleaned up in an optimum manner and then set free to operate according to its nature, with an international organization as a regulating mechanism. The Subcommittee on Security Problems made certain proposals supplementing the foregoing: it proposed that in the transition period, before the international organization possessed sufficient military strength to enforce its decrees, the major powers should act as a police force and

[20] See above, p. 6.
[21] For a detailed account of the planning of such an international organization during this period, see Russell, *op.cit.*, Chap. 2 *et seq.*

PRE-PEARL HARBOR PLANS FOR PEACE

maintain security by enforcing the armistice and the treaty limitations upon armaments.

The postwar world was thus conceived as a two-bloc system, of which one bloc was made up of the principal victorious powers and the other consisted of the remaining states. It was assumed that the latter would not only accept but even welcome the assumption of responsibility for the peace by the Great Powers until the establishment of an international organization in which all states would be represented.[22] The Subcommittee on Security Problems, which, interestingly enough, was the only subcommittee to include War and Navy Department representatives, also proposed that Germany and Japan be required to surrender unconditionally.[23]

In planning beyond the immediate issue of disarmament of the enemy, the Subcommittee indicated its belief that the ultimate peace and security of the world depended on economic well-being, involving the familiar questions of trade-barrier reduction, financial stability, and the like. On the other hand, the Territorial Subcommittee was concerned with the possibility that postwar territorial settlements would become the issue most likely to divide the wartime coalition. Consequently it stressed the preparation of alternative solutions in order to counteract any danger of division among the victorious powers, as well as to make allowances for new forces and ideas stirring in the world. As a method of arriving at final decisions it recommended a "diplomacy of principle," in which moral norms would replace power politics (a recommendation with a Wilsonian ring).[24]

[22] PWFPP, p. 12. The idea of an interim police force, incidentally, also appealed to President Roosevelt. See Sumner Welles, *Where Are We Heading?*, New York, Harper, 1946, p. 4.

[23] The Chairman of the Subcommittee, Norman Davis, communicated this line of thought to the President. However, it had not been recommended that the policy of unconditional surrender be announced formally, as in fact occurred at the meeting at Casablanca. (PWFPP, p. 127.)

[24] *Ibid.*, p. 123.

The Division of Special Research, during this period, attempted to view current military and diplomatic events in such a manner as to foresee the important problems at the end of the war and to plan for political stability on a rational basis. One of the studies begun by the Division was a catalogue of all commitments up to that time stemming from the Atlantic Charter, so that the American case could be prepared "with a full knowledge of the position of all the litigants."[25] This, incidentally, was one of the purposes of the House Inquiry during World War I, and the phrase is Wilson's.

Two essential assumptions underlay the work of the Advisory Committee and its subcommittees. The first was the familiar one that the major powers of the coalition, including the Soviet Union, would continue to act in concert after the total defeat of the Axis powers. Thus, in March 1942, the Economic Reconstruction Subcommittee had already decided that the four major powers—the United States, Great Britain, the USSR, and China—would serve cooperatively as a steering committee in a United Nations meeting on relief matters.[26] Again the Security Subcommittee postulated that the four powers would cooperate in policing the world in the interim between winning the war and the establishment of a strong international organization. This was not merely a case of wishful thinking on the part of the Subcommittee members, since it was generally believed that such cooperation was in the interest of all the victors. In particular, postwar fears at

[25] *Ibid.*, p. 150.
[26] Harley Notter, in chronicling the postwar planning of the Department of State, pointed to this decision as "the first concrete manifestation of the concept of major-power collaboration in postwar preparations directed toward the formulation of proposals for consideration by the other United Nations. This concept, which both reflected and to a degree defined the respective relations and roles of the major powers and of the other United Nations as these were being established by the war itself, developed in due course into a fixed policy with respect to the establishment not only of transitional but of permanent international organizations." (PWFPP, pp. 87-88.)

that time naturally clustered around the current enemies, and the central concern was to prevent them, once defeated, from threatening the world again with their remaining strength or rearming. Since it was clearly to Russia's interest to prevent the resurgence of Germany, the assumption of Russian cooperation in military occupation and armament supervision seemed reasonable.

A second fundamental assumption was that the United States would assume its share of the responsibility for making a just postwar settlement and would commit its military and economic resources to this end. This was, of course, a radical break with the isolationist tradition in United States foreign policy, and it was thought that the greatest obstacle to the plans of the Advisory Committee would be opposition from interest groups and doctrinaire isolationists in the United States Congress. Consequently, much attention was given to the means for convincing American public opinion of the necessity of assuming full responsibility corresponding to its new role in the international scene.

CHAPTER II

PLANNING FOR PEACE DURING WARTIME

As 1943 wore on and peace could logically be envisaged, Hull believed the time had come to realize more concretely the preliminary planning of his department. Consequently, in July, he disbanded the Advisory Committee and its subcommittees, stating that "Work has reached a point at which it is imperative that the results of our discussions to date be brought together in the form of documents which can serve as a basis of a more specific consideration of policies and proposals."[1] He still did not think that final commitments should be entered into, but that the assumptions upon which the planning was predicated ought to be fully understood and verified by the major powers involved. The wartime coalition was showing serious strains (the Russian demand for a second front, the Polish dispute, Russia's reluctance to report the existence of American aid to its population, the Italian surrender), and the Secretary felt that an atmosphere more favorable to the harmonious conclusion of his postwar plans must be created by diplomatic and economic means. He believed that the incipient friction between the Allies could be lessened by better and more careful diplomatic preparation and readiness to make decisions,[2] and that this should be done before the end of the war had arrived with its even more divisive pressures.

Since March of 1943, when Eden had visited Washington, Hull had tried to gain consensus for his plans. But he had not had a completely free hand. Eden had spent much time at the White House with Franklin Roosevelt and Hopkins, and their planning did not always proceed as Hull might

[1] PWFPP, p. 164.
[2] *Ibid.*, p. 163.

have hoped. In fact, many of the assumptions out of which the Chief Executive and Eden built their agreement must have run counter to Hull's conception of international dealings. Eden, for example, had indicated to Roosevelt that Russia would most probably be adamant concerning the incorporation of the Baltic states into the Soviet Union as part of its political sphere of influence. Roosevelt did not like the idea, but if it indeed proved inevitable, he was willing to use it as a bargaining counter for other concessions from Russia.[3]

This position must have been especially disturbing to Hull and the planners of his Territorial Subcommittee, who had envisaged the settlements as proceeding via the "diplomacy of principle," in which moral disinterestedness replaced power politics. Furthermore, Eden explained that Britain would like a strong rearmed France and Poland as balancers of the Continent. This, while distasteful enough to Roosevelt, must have been particularly so to Hull, who specifically abhorred the idea of a new system of balanced nation-states in place of his vision of a mutual security system based on the collective responsibility of the major powers.

On this question of security there also developed some friction between the White House and Mr. Hull. Roosevelt, backed by Welles (and this was one of the major contentions between Welles and Hull), initially agreed with Great Britain that the new international organization might be developed on regional lines, whereas Hull insisted upon a universal system of sovereign states. It seemed reasonable to him that Russia would cooperate in such a scheme. In Hull's view there were but two alternatives for Russia at this stage: either isolation with armaments retention or a meeting of responsibilities "under a sane, practical policy of international cooperation." Eden conceded that there were no other choices.

[3] Robert E. Sherwood, *Roosevelt and Hopkins: An Intimate History*, New York, Harper, 1948, p. 709.

Therefore, Hull felt strongly that the time had come to make the most ardent representations to the Soviet Union to work intimately with the Western democracies and with the fourth Great Power, China.

That China should be represented was most important to the President and his Secretary of State. Roosevelt told Eden that "China might become a very useful power in the Far East to help police Japan and that he wanted to strengthen China in every possible way."[4] Hull believed that the very continuity of our historical policy toward China demanded Great Power status for her. Churchill's and Eden's rejoinders[5] concerning the actual weakness of China, her anticipated instability at the end of the war, and her involvement in a revolution did not seem to the American officials to represent an honest evaluation of the situation. On the contrary, there was a tendency to interpret all such protestations as arising out of British colonial ambitions. Hull also believed that they were attempts at scuttling his proposed trusteeship plans for the Far East. Nevertheless, on March 27, 1943, at a White House Conference, with Eden in attendance, agreement seems to have been reached concerning the participation of China as one of the four Great Powers. Furthermore, postwar policies for the Far East were discussed, and the President suggested that a trusteeship be set up for Indochina, that Manchuria and Formosa be returned to China, that Korea be placed under an international trusteeship (with China, the United States, and one or two other countries participating), and that the Japanese mandated islands be internationalized.[6]

Roosevelt did, however, envisage the policing of strong points throughout the world by strong powers. Thus he seemed to recognize, even if subconsciously, that there were in fact pragmatic spheres of influence, since he assumed that those

[4] *Ibid.*, p. 716.
[5] Eden also commented that he "did not much like the idea of the Chinese running up and down the Pacific." (*Ibid.*)
[6] *Memoirs*, p. 1596.

nations which had troops and interests in certain regions of the world would also be responsible for those regions. Thus, the United States, for example, would police Formosa. It seemed to be taken for granted that the Pacific and Far East were primarily an American zone of interest.[7] Nevertheless, despite the fact that Russia had early announced her intentions regarding her interest in the Balkan states, there was no attempt either by the President or by Eden to relocate troops in Europe or the Far East to gain political advantage, nor did the Department of State conceive of such actions.

The Four-Nation Declaration

Throughout the early summer Hull continued to perfect and to communicate his plan for international cooperation. He emphasized it to Churchill and to Litvinov in March and May. In May also, Hull's senior advisory group expressed the belief that the primary issues concerning postwar policy were those of international security and organization, and they considered issuance of a declaration by the major powers concerning their intentions on these issues. When, as a result of the military decisions at the Trident Conference, the Big Three cordiality of early summer turned to discord, Hull seems not to have been particularly daunted in his plans for mutual cooperation. In fact, he appears to have thought that now more than ever was the time to prepare a healing statement. If such a pronouncement could be written, agreed to, and publicly proclaimed, Hull believed that a major step toward the fact of cooperation would have been achieved.

Work on the document, which later became the Four-Nation Declaration, was therefore intensified, and in August, at the Quebec Conference, Hull gained British approval of his draft. This was the "first occasion for the presentation by the Depart-

[7] According to Hopkins, Eden had hoped that the Japanese mandated islands would be turned over to the United States in outright ownership, whereas the President felt that they should be under a trusteeship. (Sherwood, *op.cit.*, p. 716.)

ment [of State] of definite policy recommendations based on the preparatory work done on postwar problems,"[8] and Hull undoubtedly believed the issues vital. Originally the document had been conceived as a treaty, but it was now considered more efficacious to promulgate it as a declaration, since it would come into effect immediately and require no ratification. The urgency with which Hull viewed the necessity for the adoption of the declaration is testimony, at least in part, to the importance he ascribed to it. He believed sincerely that acceptance of the terms of the document was really necessary for the successful execution of his postwar plans, and that once agreement was obtained among the Big Four it would actually cement *de facto* the stated relationships.

At Quebec, not only Hull but also the executive and military departments in general (as evidenced by a document introduced by Hopkins from "a very high level United States military strategic estimate"[9]) judged the friendship and cooperation of Russia to be of prime importance. Russia, it was estimated, would be the overriding power in Europe once Germany was defeated, with no opposing balancer, and therefore it was "essential to develop and maintain the most friendly relations." Furthermore, it was greatly desired to induce Russia to participate as an ally in the war against Japan, a factor which it was thought would materially cut our losses there. When word came from Stalin toward the end of the Conference that he would consent to a Foreign Ministers' meeting in Moscow, Allied confidence in a cooperative venture was renewed.

As an indication of the willingness of the American people to fulfill their part of the collaborative effort, Hull was much encouraged by the statement issued at Mackinac Island by a conference of Republican leaders, endorsing United States participation in a postwar international organization. When this statement was followed by the Fulbright Resolution of

[8] PWFPP, p. 187.
[9] Sherwood, *op.cit.*, p. 748.

PLANNING FOR PEACE DURING WARTIME

September 21, 1943, declaring that the House (the Senate concurring) favored the creation of appropriate international machinery with power adequate to establish and to maintain a just and lasting peace, and that it favored participation by the United States through its constitutional processes, Hull believed that one of his prime objectives was close to accomplishment. He likewise construed the Connally Resolution of 1943 as an endorsement of his postwar plans. This resolution pledged the United States, acting through its constitutional processes, to participate in an international organization based on the principle of sovereign equality. When, finally, both political parties came out with planks favoring an international organization, Hull was "greatly encouraged." He felt much relieved that one of the major obstacles, in his opinion, to a lasting international peace—namely, American isolationism—was being successfully overcome. Feeling reasonably secure of American sentiment, he applied himself more diligently than ever to the creation of an international atmosphere of cooperation among the Big Four.

The Four-Nation Declaration finally emerged from the Moscow Conference of Foreign Ministers (October 19-30, 1943) as "Declaration of Four Nations on General Security, November 1, 1943." It confirmed Hull's optimistic views about the future relations of the four powers. To Eden and Molotov, he had confided that he envisaged cooperation among Russia, the United Kingdom, and the United States on an entirely equal footing and with no secrets between any two of the nations. To the public Hull announced: "As the provisions of the Four-Nation Declaration are carried into effect, there will no longer be need for spheres of influence, for alliances, for balance of power, or any other of the special arrangements through which, in the unhappy past, the nations strove to safeguard their security or to promote their interests."[10]

[10] *Memoirs*, pp. 1314-15.

PLANNING FOR PEACE DURING WARTIME

The provisions upon which Hull so firmly placed his faith declared that the United States, the United Kingdom, the Soviet Union, and China would continue to cooperate after the conclusion of the war "for the organization and maintenance of peace and security"; that they would act together in all matters relating to the surrender and disarmament of a common enemy; that after termination of hostilities they would employ their military forces within territories of other states only for such purposes as were envisaged by this declaration and after joint consultation; and that they recognized the necessity of establishing a general international organization, based on the principle of the sovereign equality of all peace-loving states, and open to membership by all such states, large and small, for the maintenance of international peace and security.

Particularly gratifying to Hull was the inclusion of China as one of the four principal powers. He had had to argue personally with a reluctant Molotov concerning this issue, and he felt that he had won. That we valued China thus was natural in view of our historic affinity to her. We had engaged in extensive missionary work there in the educational, medical, and religious fields. We had strongly supported the Open Door and the territorial and administrative integrity of China, a policy which, while perhaps widely misrepresented and misinterpreted, to most Americans and particularly to Congress conjured up a picture of safeguarding China from the eager grasp of competing avaricious powers busily dividing China among their exclusive spheres of influences. We finally had been forced into a war in our struggle with Japan in regard to China.

Hull had consistently attempted to shore up China by all means in his power. When T. V. Soong complained about China's exclusion from the inner circle of the Combined Chiefs of Staff, Hull had been soothing. Despite his annoyance at the flouting of procedural protocol on the part of his Chinese friends in continually by-passing the Department of State in order to plead for aid and influence in the various Treasury,

War, and Navy offices,[11] he never faltered in his belief that the United States should do everything in its power to assist China to become strong and stable. When Hull had been unable to render material aid, he substituted moral aid. Thus he supported the renunciation by the United States of its extraterritorial rights in China (January 1943) and the repeal of the Chinese Exclusion Laws (December 1943). But even in times of stability the opportunities for using moral aid to gain political ends are small; and in the highly charged atmosphere of China in the early 1940's such aid could have little force.

Then, as well as in the years thereafter, Hull worked under the assumption that "Japan would disappear as a great Oriental power for a long time to come. Therefore, the only major strictly Oriental power would be China. The United States, Britain, and Russia were also Pacific powers, but the greater interests of each were elsewhere. Consequently, if there was ever to be stability in the Far East, it had to be assured with China at the center of any arrangement that was made."[12] Furthermore, despite the adverse reports which must have reached him, Hull felt that the government of Chiang Kai-shek was the proper representative of the Chinese people. Chiang Kai-shek, in Hull's opinion, "had followed faithfully in the footsteps of Sun Yat-sen in attempting . . . the creation of a real Republic out of the innumerable divisions and subdivisions composing the vast territory of China. He was wise and patriotic. He knew the Chinese people."[13] When Stalin not only agreed to allow China to be classed among the leading powers of the world, but also promised that he would enter the war against Japan as soon as the German forces were beaten, Hull was deeply gratified.

During the fall of 1943, several new committees were formed in the Department of State to concentrate on possible postwar

[11] Hull rather blamed the President for allowing these conditions to continue. (*Ibid.*, p. 1587.)
[12] *Ibid.*
[13] *Ibid.*, p. 1586.

problems. The immediate impetus for their formation had been the necessity of a position vis-à-vis Stalin at the Moscow Conference, particularly on territorial problems. These committees were organized on either a country or an area basis, depending upon the region, and for the Far East an area committee was deemed most advisable. Stanley K. Hornbeck was named the Chairman and George H. Blakeslee the alternate. However, once again the self-imposed moratorium on all decisions concerning boundaries and related questions hindered the formulation of specific recommendations.

The seeming success of the Moscow Conference also infected the Cairo and Teheran discussions of the heads of state. There, Roosevelt similarly reassured Chiang of the Great Power status of China. At the expense of annoying the British, who consistently felt that Roosevelt overrated the Chinese alliance, Chiang was promised more British and American military aid (particularly in clearing Burma)[14] and was supported in his territorial desires. The Cairo Declaration duly announced that the three great allies—the United States, China, and the United Kingdom—were fighting to restrain and punish the aggression of Japan. None coveted gain for themselves, nor entertained thoughts of territorial expansion. However, Japan was to be stripped of all the islands she had seized or occupied in the Pacific since 1914, as well as of all territories she had taken from China. Manchuria, Formosa, and the Pescadores were specifically to be returned to the Republic of China. In due course, Korea was also promised freedom. Finally, the Allies promised to persevere until they procured unconditional surrender.

Stalin again pledged his support in the Far Eastern campaign as soon as Germany was beaten and he could transport

[14] However, the British did not in the end acquiesce in this demand, and Chiang was therefore misinformed. Cf. William Hardy McNeill, *America, Britain and Russia: Their Co-operation and Conflict, 1941-1946*, London and New York, Oxford University Press, 1953, p. 347.

PLANNING FOR PEACE DURING WARTIME

his troops across the country. That there might be a price attached was considered, and much of the Yalta accord was anticipated at Teheran.[15] It seems that the terms had previously been discussed with Chiang, and had not met with disapproval.[16] In fact, Roosevelt reported to the Pacific War Council, of which China was a member, that "it was gratifying to him to find that Marshal Stalin and the Generalissimo saw eye to eye with him on all the major problems of the Pacific. Therefore he felt it would not be hard to reach arrangements about the control of the Pacific after the defeat of Japan."[17] One further important result of the Teheran Conference was that Roosevelt temporarily wrested for China a place as one of the Four Policemen of the postwar world, a victory which undoubtedly pleased Hull.

Plans for the Postwar World

As 1944 approached, victory could be envisaged in the near future, and the Department of State moved toward advanced preparations for the postwar world. On January 15, 1944, Hull reorganized the pertinent agencies in the State Department.[18] In particular, reliance for postwar policy was shifted from the somewhat informal Advisory Group to two newly established committees—namely, the Policy Committee, which was to focus on immediate problems regarding foreign policy, and the Postwar Programs Committee, charged with formulating postwar plans. However, as the year progressed it was found more and more that the two committees often dealt with the same subject matter, and that current policy tended to influence future policy. Hence the committees frequently met together.

It fell to the Postwar Programs Committee to write major policy papers on twenty-six outstanding fields of investigation. Most important of these were the treatment of enemy countries and their terms of surrender, reparations, control, and so

[15] Feis, *The China Tangle*, p. 113.
[16] *Ibid.*
[17] *Ibid.*
[18] Departmental Order 1218.

forth. Japan was very much in the forefront of these investigations, with detailed papers on plans for a military government for Japan as well as territorial settlements. While these papers have not yet been made public, it is safe to assume that the overall concept which guided the planners was an adherence to four-power postwar agreement and cooperation. In a major policy address, explaining the postwar thinking to the public, Hull stated on April 4: "However difficult the road may be, there is no hope of turning victory into enduring peace unless the real interests of this country, the British Commonwealth, the Soviet Union, and China are harmonized and unless they agree and act together. This is the solid framework upon which all future policy and international organization must be built." He went on to warn that "for these powers to become divided in their aims and fail to recognize and harmonize their basic interests can produce only disaster. . . ."[19] More particularly, in response to a request by the Civil Affairs Division of the War Department and the Occupied Areas Section of the Navy Department, as early as February 1944 the Department of State began to draft policy statements on twenty crucial questions concerning the occupation of Japan and Korea. The job fell mainly to the Interdivisional Area Committee on the Far East, but its conclusions were reviewed by the Postwar Programs Committee.

The postwar objectives as envisaged at that time are noteworthy in that they prejudiced later planning to a marked degree. In fact, their basic conception was not modified until well into the chill of the Cold War. Japan, in this formulation, was to be prevented from ever again menacing the United States and the other countries of the Pacific, and in order to achieve this objective a government which would respect the rights of other states was to be instituted. This in turn was envisaged in three distinct stages. The first demanded a complete subordination of Japan to the immediate terms of sur-

[19] PWFPP, p. 234.

render (which at that time were stated as "unconditional surrender") with retribution for military aggression (presumably, heavy reparations). The second stage still involved a close surveillance of Japan, but as she showed herself worthy of trust she was to be allowed some relaxation from the victor's control. Finally, in the third period, the ultimate aim of the United States was to be realized—namely, that Japan would properly discharge her responsibilities in a peaceful family of nations. Furthermore, the Cairo Declaration was reaffirmed as the definitive statement concerning territorial settlements, and Japan was also to be completely demilitarized. After this initial demilitarization, however, democratization of its populace was to be furthered, for only in this way could militarism be finally eradicated. And, to forestall desperation on the part of the vanquished nation, Japan would eventually be allowed a share in the world economy to a degree compatible with international security.

It is not surprising that the representatives of the three departments, in presenting their views of the cardinal problems of the occupation and post-occupation era, should disagree at various points. On January 5, 1945, the State-War-Navy Coordinating Committee (SWNCC), which had been formed in December of 1944, created a subcommittee charged with consideration of post-hostility problems and the reconciliation of the views of the three departments.[20] This committee, often relying upon previous State documents, then prepared the basic policy papers in regard to Japan. Its decisions were reviewed by SWNCC as a whole, or even by the President, before they became United States policy.

Having met at least once a week since February, the committee had, by July 1945, a basic directive for the occupation of Japan. This had been formulated upon the premise that Japan would mirror the German situation, and that there

[20] Cf. Hugh Borton, "United States Occupation Policies in Japan Since Surrender," *Political Science Quarterly*, LXII, No. 2 (June 1947), pp. 250-57.

would be a military government, rather than use being made of the administrative machinery of the Japanese government which, as it turned out, was retained after the Potsdam Declaration.[21] Japan still had 5,000,000 troops in the field, many of whom had given good evidence of patriotic will to resist to the very end, and it was understandable that our primary preoccupation at that time was with military analyses and unconditional military subjugation. At Yalta a few advisors had already intimated that perhaps we did not need to rely on Russian aid to subdue the Japanese and therefore should not play the too eager solicitor, but General Marshall and the army intelligence felt that an invasion of Japan was inevitable, and that the more aid the United States could obtain in this endeavor, the more speedily the bloody enterprise would be concluded. Therefore, the planning for an all-out invasion with the aid of the Russians excluded for all practical purposes a political settlement with Japan.

It is quite true that, in the spring of 1945, several of the highest ranking policy-makers began to question the meaning of "unconditional surrender" in regard to Japan. At a State-War-Navy meeting on May 1, Secretary of the Navy Forrestal turned attention to the political objectives in the Far East.[22] Now that peace had come to Europe and the end of the war could be envisaged, the Secretary began to wonder about the power relationships to come. How thoroughly did we want to beat Japan, and did we wish to "Morgenthau" her as we planned to do with Germany? Who in the Far East should counterbalance Russia after the war, China or Japan? And did we contemplate readmission of Japan to the family of nations after she had been demilitarized? Forrestal felt that our planning concerning these most crucial political objectives, including

[21] Cf. Edwin M. Martin, *The Allied Occupation of Japan*, Stanford, Calif., Stanford University Press, 1948, pp. 6-7.
[22] See *The Forrestal Diaries*, ed. by Walter Millis, New York, Viking Press, 1951, p. 52.

the future power relationships, was thoroughly inadequate, if indeed it existed at all.

It was perhaps symptomatic of the narrow range of communication among the various policy-forming committees of the Department of State that the Secretary of the Navy should feel that we had paid little attention to the real postwar formulations. In a speech some years later, Forrestal declared that our "diplomatic planning of the peace was far below the quality of planning that went into the conduct of the war. We regarded the war, broadly speaking, as a ball game which we had to finish as quickly as possible, but in doing so there was comparatively little thought as to the relationships between nations which would exist after Germany and Japan were destroyed."[23]

One must assume that there was some dissension and vagueness in the Far East Subcommittee of SWNCC concerning our objectives in Japan. The military members obviously looked toward a total defeat by military measures, including an invasion, and concerned themselves with such factors as "wake of battle" occupations prior to final surrender, and other ultimate battle conditions. The Department of State members, on the other hand, were more inclined to consider the meaning of unconditional surrender as encompassing the unconditional dissipation of the Japanese militaristic enterprise, but felt that the means by which this was to be achieved did not necessarily have to be military encounters alone. If the liberal elements of Japan could be strengthened to such a degree as to make possible Japan's surrender without an invasion, so much the better.

Could unconditional surrender mean that Japan would be allowed to keep her emperor system? This is precisely the point upon which there was most disagreement among our policy planners. Grew, who in his long tenure as Ambassador to Japan had learned to know the Japanese well, argued that one could, indeed, construe unconditional surrender to mean

[23] *Ibid.*, p. 53.

the complete subjugation of the military machine but still allow a role to the Emperor, particularly if he could be of potential use to the Americans. Throughout the war, Grew had taken the position that American propaganda ought not attack the Emperor himself, since the Emperor had been a tool and not an instigator in the complicities of the militaristic party and that it was only the Emperor who through an Imperial Rescript could definitively end the ghastly struggle. And now that the war was in its final stages, Grew felt that a declaration by the United States to the effect that Japan's religious system would not be eradicated and that Japan would be allowed to continue her emperor tradition would greatly strengthen the liberal party. In fact it might even initiate a surrender offer. In particular, Grew believed that such an offer should be made prior to invasion and immediately after our bombing of Japan by the B-29's. Once Japan was desperate, once the last-ditch fight had begun, Grew thought there would be little chance for any rational surrender. However, if she was given a taste of our strength and also an indication of our fair-minded interpretation of unconditional surrender, she might feel she could honorably accept our terms. President Truman, in a speech on May 8, had already stated that unconditional surrender did not mean the extermination or enslavement of the Japanese people, and Grew felt there would be no harm in amplifying this statement and declaring precisely what we meant. Of course there were opponents of this policy, who either thought that such a course would indicate to the Japanese that we were weak, or who considered it outright appeasement.

Nevertheless, Grew, as Acting Secretary of State, acquainted Truman with his ideas on May 28, 1945, and repeated his views to the Secretaries of War, Navy, and the Chiefs of Staff on May 29. According to Grew, the President agreed with his position (Forrestal denies this), as did the military leaders, but owing to undisclosed military reasons the Joint Chiefs of Staff did not want such a statement at this time. Later Grew

PLANNING FOR PEACE DURING WARTIME

thought that the fighting on Okinawa, which was then in progress, accounted for the military reasons, and that a declaration of the kind which Grew had envisaged (and which was actually made at the Potsdam meeting, with of course the deletion of the reference to the Emperor) would have indicated to the Japanese some American weakness. Timing was thus alleged to have scuttled Grew's plan.

Stimson and Forrestal also favored Grew's approach and met several times during June and July to discuss further the meaning and execution of unconditional surrender. On June 18 Grew again saw the President and urged that the draft of the Japanese surrender ultimatum be released as soon as the fall of Okinawa should be announced. The President said he liked the idea, but since the Big Three Conference was so soon to convene, he thought he might want to discuss the issue there. Whereas Grew felt that there should be an announcement immediately, many of the policy planners did not display a similar sense of urgency. Few of the military planners at that time really thought the Japanese would surrender without an invasion of their homeland, and since the target date for the invasion was to be November 1, 1945, there was little inclination to believe that surrender was an immediate problem. Furthermore, there were still many people who truly believed that we should await the Russian entry into the war.

Harriman and a few other planners were beginning to advocate the view that Russia was far more eager to enter the war in Asia than we were to have her enter, and that indeed it would in all probability be to our advantage if we could end the struggle before Russia made a token contribution and then demanded substantial rewards; but they were in the minority. Byrnes[24] and Truman seemed to feel that one of the major purposes of the Potsdam Conference would be to get the Rus-

[24] Byrnes, despite the fact that he also seemed very anxious to have Russia commit her forces in the Far Eastern struggle, also told Forrestal that he hoped to have the Japanese affair over with before the Russians got in. (*Ibid.*, p. 78.)

37

PLANNING FOR PEACE DURING WARTIME

sians into the Japanese war,[25] and in fact American delegates attending the Conference were believed by Forrestal and Grew to be so unfavorably disposed toward the further clarification of the unconditional surrender concept that the draft of the Proclamation might be "ditched" on the way over to Potsdam.[26]

Grew, who did not go to Potsdam, and Forrestal, who attended but without an invitation, must have placed their hopes on Stimson, for they knew that he was perhaps more interested in the viability of the Proclamation than almost anyone else. He, in particular, had intimate knowledge of the long development of the atom bomb, and one may surmise that he was particularly anxious to obtain a surrender on a political basis, knowing what devastation would be in store for Japan. On July 2, Stimson had written a memorandum to the President embodying the same principles which Grew advocated, including the suggestion of the retention of the Emperor. But Byrnes, upon the advice of Hull, had the reference to the Emperor deleted on July 17.[27]

Byrnes is believed to have ordered the deletion because he felt that too many Americans had made disparaging remarks about the Emperor, and that an avowal to keep him now might embarrass these officials. Whether this deletion was a cardinal error, as has often been claimed since,[28] is not definitively ascertainable; yet one must seriously consider the opinions of Grew, Stimson, and Forrestal, who felt that the war might have been ended in May, June, or July, before the entrance of Russia and before the dropping of the atom bombs, if the unconditional surrender statement had contained the stipulation that the Emperor would be allowed some status subject to the Supreme Commander's authority, even as the final terms of surrender actually did.[29] That Japan was already at

[25] *Ibid.*   [26] *Ibid.*, pp. 73-74.   [27] Cf. *Memoirs*, p. 1594.
[28] See, e.g., Hanson W. Baldwin, *Great Mistakes of the War*, New York, Harper, 1950, pp. 92, 95.
[29] The Department of State already had a draft of the Proclamation in May that was identical, apart from a few stylistic changes, with the

38

the point of exhaustion in July should perhaps have been evident to us from our interception of the Japanese coded messages to Russia asking her to intercede with the West for peace. It was later confirmed from documents and evidences examined after the war's end.[30]

The Potsdam Proclamation (popularly known as the Potsdam Declaration) issued on July 26 was one of the important documents referred to again and again in the drafting of the Japanese peace treaty. It was signed only by three powers, the United States, Britain, and China, since Russia had not yet entered the war and was still waiting for the expiration period of her Neutrality Pact with Japan. However, Russia adhered to it subsequently.

The substance of the document, after stating that the Allies were fully determined to subdue Japan in case she continued her ill-advised resistance, was that the irresponsible militarists under whose authority Japan had embarked on world conquest would have to be eliminated and that Japan would be occupied until a new order had been established there, and until Japan's war-making capacity had been destroyed. Furthermore, the Cairo Declaration was reaffirmed, and notice was given that Japan would be limited to the four large islands and such minor ones as the Allies determined. On the other hand, the Allies indicated that they by no means intended to destroy the Japanese as a nation. They promised that the military forces after disarmament would be allowed to lead peaceful and productive lives in Japan. They intended just punishment for war criminals, but their policy in regard to the remainder of the country would be to revive democratic tendencies and to establish freedom of speech, religion, and thought and respect for the fundamental human rights. They would

---

final Proclamation (before the provision regarding the Emperor had been deleted).

[30] On this general subject, see Robert J. C. Butow, *Japan's Decision to Surrender*, Stanford, Calif., Stanford University Press, 1954.

permit Japan access to raw materials and an industrial capacity concomitant with a peacetime economy. Eventually, Japan would again be allowed to trade in the world market. As soon as these objectives had been attained, and Japan had established a peaceful and responsible government, in accordance with the freely expressed will of the Japanese people, the occupying forces were to be removed. Finally, the instrument again called for the "unconditional surrender of all Japanese armed forces," and threatened prompt and utter destruction in case of non-compliance.

It is well known that the Japanese reaction to the offer was interpreted as a rejection, the atom bombs were dropped, and Russia entered the war against Japan. On the morning of August 10, however, the Japanese sued for peace under the terms of the Potsdam Declaration, "with the understanding that the said Declaration does not comprise any demand which prejudices the prerogatives of His Majesty as a Sovereign Ruler." Byrnes reports that he told the President: "I do not see why we should retreat from our demand for unconditional surrender. That demand was presented to Japan before the use of the bomb and before the Soviet Union was a belligerent. If any conditions are to be accepted, I want the United States and not Japan to state the conditions."[81] The President agreed and asked Byrnes to draft a reply, which stated:

> From the moment of surrender, the authority of the Emperor and the Japanese Government to rule the state shall be subject to the Supreme Commander of the Allied powers who will take such steps as he deems proper to effectuate the surrender terms.
>
> The Emperor will be required to authorize and ensure the signature by the Government of Japan and the Japanese Imperial General Headquarters of the surrender terms necessary to carry out the provisions of the Potsdam Declaration. . . .
>
> The ultimate form of government of Japan shall, in accordance

[81] James F. Byrnes, *Speaking Frankly*, New York, Harper, 1947, p. 209.

PLANNING FOR PEACE DURING WARTIME

with the Potsdam Declaration, be established by the freely expressed will of the people.[82]

Whether the final communiqué from Secretary Byrnes was not really an acceptance of a conditional surrender of the type which Grew would have considered sufficient in May and which Stimson advocated in July is debatable; nevertheless Byrnes convinced himself that the notion of unconditional surrender had not been violated. Consequently, on August 14, the Japanese accepted the Potsdam surrender with Byrnes' clarification of the 11th, and the fighting ceased. General MacArthur, as Supreme Commander for the Allied Powers, then accepted the surrender aboard the "Missouri" on September 2.

At Potsdam, also, Secretary Byrnes planned for the peace treaties with the belligerents, and later made the comment that the first aim of the conference was to set up "the machinery and the procedures for the earliest possible drafting and completion of peace treaties."[83]

[82] *Ibid.*, pp. 209-10.
[83] *Ibid.*, pp. 67-68.

CHAPTER III

PEACE-MAKING AND THE COLD WAR

WE HAVE SEEN that, during the period up to 1945, the postwar planning of the State Department was in large measure influenced by assumptions about the nature of the international system that had been carried over from a prior stage of the nation's diplomatic history. These premises, so far as they were ever valid, were clearly becoming outmoded by the revolutionary changes going on in the world, yet it took a long time to modify them to accord more closely with the realities of the day.

The assumptions reflected the secure position which the United States had enjoyed in the late nineteenth and early twentieth centuries because of its insular geographical position and the British control of the seas. These meant that the United States did not have to be greatly concerned about her defense position or the size of her armed forces in peacetime. It suited her far better to believe in a world in which the conduct of nations was guided more by rules of law and morality than by force.

After two world wars, however, the security position of the United States had entirely changed. The surrounding oceans no longer offered her adequate protection, and the declining power of the British Empire compelled her to rely more on her own strength. Furthermore, it was becoming clear by 1945 that the world was going through a period in which the rule of law was of declining influence in controlling the conduct of states. In order to know what the national interest had now become, it was necessary to take a very realistic view of what the actual behavior of nations was likely to be in the postwar world, and to mark out the course of United States policy accordingly.

PEACE-MAKING AND THE COLD WAR

This "realistic" approach was evolved fitfully, with contributions from many points of view which were not easily harmonized. Nevertheless, most of the participants in the decisions of the time tended to accept the following propositions: that neither the innate goodness of mankind nor the harmony of interests of nations guaranteed universal respect for international law and justice; that therefore the primary requisite was to maintain a strong military force even in time of peace; that in view of the rapid changes in military technology the safety of the United States could no longer be sustained in isolation but required allies abroad; that economic and ideological weapons were also necessary in the maintenance of national power; and that in preserving the hard core of the national interest it is often necessary to sacrifice more contingent national values.

The moralism, isolationism, utopianism, and rejection of military power in peacetime which had been thought by many to characterize American opinion on international matters were far from dominant after World War II. Thus isolationism was discredited to the extent that American entrance into the United Nations ran into little opposition and in fact was supported by Congressional initiative. "Back to normalcy" was again a popular sentiment, but it appeared to be merely a nonpolitical desire for the pleasures of peace and was not this time elevated to an ideology or political program. Even the temporary acquiescence in a program of cooperation with the Soviet Union, which is often cited as evidence of postwar utopianism, can readily be interpreted in more realistic terms —namely, that it was a calculated risk based on the premise that no obvious reason existed for war between the major victorious powers.

Evidence that opinion in this country had become more realistic after World War II is found in the reaction of the nation when the hostility of the Soviet Union became manifest. The mounting anti-Soviet consensus in the United States was not surprising, nor was it *per se* indicative of a new realism. After all, the time of the Red scare had not long passed, and the groups which had once felt a fear of domestic communism were naturally suspicious of Soviet communism. The significant fact was not the consensus of public opinion against the USSR, but the growing willingness in time of peace to make large sacrifices in order to be able to confront hostile powers from a position of military strength.

We may say, therefore, that from 1947 onward the government of the United States, with widespread popular support, displayed a strong and increasing willingness to follow a policy of *Realpolitik* in international affairs in promoting our national interests. At the same time, there was no consensus as to how to do so. A consensus on the means of *Realpolitik* presupposes, in the first place, a common conception of the national interest on the part of the decision-makers. Everyone agreed, of course, that the central aim was national survival, with our form of government and way of life remaining intact. Nevertheless, in a heterogeneous, democratic society, the aims of national existence are bound to be construed in different ways, and it is easy for any one of many groups to elevate its own economic or ideological concern to the status of national interest.

Secondly, a consensus on how to practice a realistic policy depends upon a common appraisal of the active and latent forces operating in the international arena at the time. There were lapses in the objectivity of our appraisal of these forces—for example, as in the case of our attitude toward China, in the years immediately preceding its loss to the Communists. There was also a tendency to believe that a realistic pursuit of the national interest precluded *any* supranational action, whereas this type of action may, under certain circumstances, be a realistic and mature way of furthering the permanent national interest.

Finally, a consensus on the practice of a realistic foreign policy presupposes a common evaluation among the decision-makers of the probable effectiveness of various strategies and instruments. But there are bound to be divergencies here because of the differences in background, experience, and training of the personnel of the various agencies engaged in making decisions. Thus, even when the State Department, the Pentagon, and the various Congressional committees are equally determined to be realistic, they may on occasion come up with quite divergent policies.

It is to be observed that the postwar aims and policies of the United States were stated more and more in terms of "security." This formula indicates a growing anxiety in the face of international forces which had for many years seemed remote but were no longer so. The formula is also an expression of that aspect of the national interest to which virtually everyone assented—namely, national survival. It is therefore to be expected that, in the analysis of any major diplomatic issue of this period, the basic problem was "How does this fit into our overall security program?" The *Realpolitik* of the period was thus essentially defensive in character, and "realism," in the various versions which were proposed, was primarily the search for a reliable strategy of security.

The evolution of our policy toward Japan during the years 1947-1950 will be considered in the following chapters from the point of view sketched above. There is much evidence that the decision-makers in our government approached the problem of Japan from a realistic viewpoint, at least in intent. Indeed, it might be argued that the suppression of hostile feelings toward Japan and the representation of our former enemies as our friends was a manifestation of *Realpolitik*, since it promised us a position of strength in the Pacific. In brief, the evolution of our postwar policy toward Japan is the development of conceptions regarding the role of Japan in our global security arrangements. In this sense the Japanese peace settlement was different from other peace treaties to which we have been a party. At the same time, various agencies—e.g., the State Department, the Defense Department, SCAP, the other nation members of the Far Eastern Commission—held quite different views on the best role for Japan. As a result, the achievement of a consistent list of desiderata for a treaty of peace was a highly complex and delicate matter, arrived at partly through discussion, persuasion, and compromise, and partly by adjustment to the pressure of external events.

Toward an Overall Foreign Policy

We have seen that when World War II was over and the time for postwar planning was at hand, the United States did not possess a clear-cut overall policy for dealing with the emerging peacetime world. Various starts had been made toward such a policy, but the top officials had been too preoccupied with the conduct of the war to give much thought to it. They were also reluctant to bring up questions during the war which might disturb our allies.

The great manifestoes of the war, especially the Atlantic Charter and the Declaration by United Nations, did indeed provide a partial statement of peacetime aims, but these were set out, for the most part, in terms of ideal goals without any specified strategy for accomplishing them.

Considerable attention had been given in the State Department to the preparation of plans for a basic instrument of a general international organization to take the place of the League of Nations. But it was not until the war was over that the President and his top advisors were able to come to any definite conclusions about such plans.

How one thought about a global postwar policy depended in large part on the image one held of the nature of the postwar system. Among the variety of possible patterns were the following: (1) enforcement of peace through an international organization, (2) maintenance of peace by balance of power,

(3) division of the world into spheres of influence, each controlled by a top power, and (4) various mixtures of these images.

Many of the planners in the State Department during the war seemed to be thinking primarily in terms of the first image. They assumed that all the principal powers would participate in some kind of a collective system and that their combined action would be sufficient to prevent future aggressions. Few of them thought in terms of a world kept at peace by a balance-of-power mechanism. Hardly any of them came out in favor of a world made up of Great Powers and spheres of influence, since this was contrary to the conception of a universal system of independent states which was a basic idea in American foreign policy. Many in fact seemed to be unaware of the image or images that shaped their planning.

Their attitudes were also influenced by their previous experience, their personal values and prejudices, and particularly their views about the Soviet Union. An expert knowledge of high international politics was not an essential requirement for holding the top posts in foreign policy-making. President Truman and Secretary of State Byrnes had been skilled politicians in domestic rather than foreign affairs. Though neither of them had been markedly isolationist before the war, they tended in their values and sympathies (especially Byrnes) to be rather more parochial than cosmopolitan. They were preoccupied with the problems of restoring the nation to a normal peacetime status. This included steps toward demobilization, peaceful settlement of disputes, and easy trade relations with other countries. They spent little time talking about the intricacies of power politics and the balancing of power.

It was with such predispositions that the early postwar experiences with Russia and the dramatic revolution in China sharply clashed. The American response to these experiences was bound to impinge heavily on the process of making peace with Japan.

The relevant events are well known. In mainland China, Mao triumphed finally and completely over the Kuomintang; in Europe and the Middle East, increasing friction with Soviet Russia concerned the postwar government of Rumania, Hungary, and Bulgaria, the Soviet attempt at subversion in Persian Azerbaijan and Greece, and particularly occupation policy in Germany. As these events unfolded, the American reaction was quite different in the Far East than in the West. There was confusion and disagreement over the nature of the Kuomintang and Mao's movement; an unrealistic attempt to reconcile irreconcilable forces, and hence American policies that were bound to fail; and, once their failure was clear, a bitter residue of disillusionment and recrimination. The West, by contrast, was a more familiar world and the United States responded to the increasingly intransigent hostility of the Soviet Union with remarkable imagination, strength, quickness, and success. The United States resumed closer cooperation with Great Britain, came forth with the Truman Doctrine and speedy aid to Greece and Turkey, established the Marshall Plan, and eventually pressed for what became the North Atlantic Treaty Organization. Indeed, by 1948, when the place of China was still obscure, the confrontation with an antagonistic USSR in Europe and the Middle East had elicited a serious attempt to formulate a new and systematic policy—the Western Cold War strategy. In particular, a new agency, the Policy Planning Staff of the State Department, was created, with George Kennan at its head, for purposes of systematic planning. Furthermore, the presence of General Marshall as Secretary of State in 1947 was of considerable importance in the achievement of a coherent strategy, since he provided a link beween the armed services and the State Department and he enjoyed the confidence of the President and Congress to an extraordinary degree.

PEACE-MAKING AND THE COLD WAR

The systematic policy for dealing with the Cold War, as developed by Truman, Marshall, Kennan, and their associates, may be summarized as follows: (1) The Soviet Union was pursuing a policy of unlimited expansionism, and the emotional and ideological roots of this policy were, at least for the present, inaccessible to reason or influence, with the consequence that only firm resistance at each point where aggression was threatened could effectively check the ambitions of the Soviet Union. (2) The line to be held against Soviet expansion was the existing boundary of the Soviet empire, not our own national borders or some intermediate line, because successful expansion up to any such line would not satisfy Soviet ambition and it might provide supplementary resources which would make the Soviet Union irresistible in an ultimate struggle. (3) Soviet expansionism could readily take the form of infiltration through local Communist parties in those nations in which economic and social conditions were bad. Consequently, a corollary to the containment of the Soviet Union was an effort to strengthen the social and economic systems of those nations which had anti-Communist governments and potentially strong Communist opposition. (4) The United States could not by itself hold the line against Soviet expansionism, for the burden would entail the transformation of its economy to a war footing; consequently, a system of alliances should be sought with nations having a common interest in resisting Soviet encroachment. (5) Although Soviet expansion was to be resisted everywhere, the defense of Europe was to have primacy. This followed logically from (2) and (4) above, since in 1947 it was considered that what Russia needed to match the United States in war potential was a large and efficient industrial establishment, which it could acquire by absorbing Central and Western Europe; and, on the other hand, the only allies which had the industrial resources to share with the United States the burden of defense against the Soviet Union were the nations of Western

Europe. (6) The foregoing strategic principles had been made necessary because the precepts of national self-determination and of world law, as proclaimed by the United Nations Charter, had been forcibly threatened. In this sense, the pursuit of certain international aims and the pursuit of national security by realistic means were reconciled.[1]

While this Cold War policy was far more systematic than the policy existing at the close of the war, there were still some intrinsic difficulties and dilemmas in it which need to be noted.

In the first place, even after deciding that Communist Russia was a menace, there remained a difficulty in assessing the real character of the threat. Was the danger primarily the Soviet Union as an imperialistic power, or was it communism as an expansionist ideology? This question did not have to be resolved so long as the system of Communist states was monolithic. But the question became important when Communist China developed as apparently an independent center of Communist power, and when Yugoslavia successfully seceded from the previously undivided Soviet system of states. If the menace was communism itself, then our Cold War strategy should be directed against every Communist state, regardless of its relations with the Soviet Union. If the menace was the expansionism of the Soviet Union, then each separate Communist state should be treated independently on its merits, and even the possibility of an alliance with one or more of them would be open. Interwoven with this strategic question was a moral one: was the Soviet menace to be regarded as evil primarily because it threatened our national existence, or because the ideology which it represented was intrinsically vicious—e.g., materialistic, anti-individualistic, atheistic, and immoral? If the former, then the principles of our Cold War policy were to be regarded as requirements of *Realpolitik*; if

[1] The list of precepts of our Cold War strategy given above is not drawn from any one source, but is suggested by official documents, the writings of men close to the centers of discussion at the time, and by the actual course of action taken by the United States government.

the latter, they were principles of a crusade. This distinction had practical consequences, for example, in deciding whether to continue economic and military aid to Yugoslavia.

Another set of difficulties resided in the estimation of the imminence and magnitude of the Soviet threat and the related calculation of the extent to which the nation must make sacrifices and rearm. Actually the sense of the urgency of the national danger did not at any time reach fever pitch. Whatever the reason and whatever the rationalizations—such as "the Russians want us to spend ourselves into bankruptcy"—it was commonly accepted that the Cold War did not call for enormous economic sacrifices on the part of the American people. In fact, many have thought that the new defense expenditures had a "pump-priming" effect which benefited the economy as a whole. Thus, the difficulty involved in estimating the imminence of the Soviet threat and the quantity of effort needed to meet it was perhaps less a difficulty of calculation than of moral decision: that is, a difficulty on the part of a free people in making real sacrifices over a long period of time, and a difficulty on the part of political leaders in committing themselves to unpopular campaigning in behalf of such sacrifices.

The principle of forming alliances in order to ensure national security contains a whole nest of difficulties. In the first place, if a nation's allies are free agents, then joint action with them necessarily limits the nation's freedom and scope of decision. On the other hand, if our allies, by one means or another, were always to be pressed into concurrence with our decisions, then the United States would be in danger of copying one of the aspects of Soviet conduct which it was most bitterly resisting, or else of repelling the Allies into neutralism. Thus there arise very delicate problems of how far to accommodate ourselves to the wishes of our allies, and how far to insist on the primacy of our own decisions. The selection of allies is complicated by hostilities among states which are remote from our immediate concern, with the result that a security agreement with one state may alienate another (e.g., the case of Pakistan and India). Our policy planners were thus confronted with the problem of arranging a hierarchy of strategic objectives, when circumstances were such that several of them, all ideally useful to our security, could not simultaneously be achieved. The principle of seeking alliances is somewhat indeterminate until such a hierarchy is worked out in detail.

CHAPTER IV

PEACE PROPOSALS: 1947-1950

THE Cold War and the fall of China to the Communists were the events which finally dominated the preparation of a peace treaty for Japan. However, the full significance of these events was not immediately clear to all those groups in the United States government and among its allies which had some influence in shaping a treaty; and even when their significance was fully understood, there was considerable disagreement on the place of Japan in an anti-Communist global strategy and on the procedures for incorporating Japan into that strategic framework. Furthermore, even though security against Communist expansionism finally became the central objective of all planning with regard to Japan, there were subsidiary objectives which the United States and its allies never ceased to pursue: the termination of financial aid to the defeated and economically prostrate nation (almost entirely an American concern), guarantees against the resurgence of Japanese imperialism (a great concern of the Pacific nations), protection against Japanese commercial competition (which worried Great Britain particularly), desire for reparations (on which the countries occupied during the war by the Japanese were particularly insistent), and other minor objectives. The present chapter is concerned with the progress made in 1947-1950 in resolving these competing objectives and strategies and designing a definite plan for a peace treaty with Japan. Although many issues remained unsettled in 1950, when Dulles was assigned the mission of negotiating the treaty, we shall find that the essential plans for the treaty were complete by that time. It is worth emphasizing at the start that the crystallization of plans for the treaty was simplified not only by concurrence in the overwhelming importance of security, but also by the assumption, which almost all the American planning groups implicitly shared, that peace with Japan was primarily an American concern.

It will be useful to begin by summarizing the proposals made in 1947 by various groups which were influential in the evolution of the treaty.

A Summary of Proposals in 1947

(1) *MacArthur*. The constellation of ideas to be found in General MacArthur's various statements concerning peace with Japan is remarkable and rather puzzling, and can be understood only in terms of his estimate of the effect of the Occupation on Japan. He maintained that "Japan today understands as thoroughly as any nation that war does not pay. Her spiritual revolution has been probably the greatest the world has ever known."[1] The renunciation of war by the Japanese was, in fact, incorporated as the famous Article 9 of the Constitution, and MacArthur insisted, and perhaps was actually convinced, that the Constitution was the free expression of the will of the people, in spite of the known circumstances of its composition and adoption. Similarly, he felt that the other reforms, originated by the Occupation authorities but later expressed in the Constitution, had taken root and would be pursued by the Japanese of their own accord. It is consistent with this estimate of the effects of the Occupation that he suggested a non-technical treaty which would affirm high ideals and purposes and would not give the impression that we repudiated the reforms we had initiated.

He recommended a quick treaty partly because prolonging the Occupation might cause the United States to seem imperialistic to the Japanese, but also because a treaty would have stimulating economic effects. As long as Japan was occupied, it would be the responsibility of the United States to

[1] Supreme Commander for the Allied Powers, Report of Government Section, *Political Reorientation of Japan: September 1945 to September 1948* (hereafter cited as *Political Reorientation of Japan*), 2 vols., Washington, D.C., G.P.O., 1959, p. 765.

maintain an adequate standard of living, and he felt that as a result the Japanese would tend to lapse into indolence, whereas the restoration of sovereignty would restore incentive and release energies.[2] MacArthur proposed rather generous terms to help Japan's economic recovery. He was opposed to stripping Japan of her industrial capacity (except for armaments and aircraft), wished to allow the Japanese to engage in shipping and shipbuilding, and was against most reparations.

MacArthur's proposals regarding post-treaty security were extremely optimistic. At one point he said that "the Japanese are relying upon the advanced spirituality of the world to protect them against undue aggression."[3] In general he remained opposed to allowing the Japanese to have any armed forces, beyond a police sufficient to deal with internal disorders. Japan, he claimed, above all wished neutrality, and should become "the Switzerland of the Pacific." He made various proposals of methods for defending Japan, but felt that the best would be defense by the United Nations.[4] Later MacArthur seems to have revised his opinion. He still felt that the peace treaty itself should not include any security provisions, but that after the treaty was signed, Japan should be invited "to assure herself of security in the Communist-threatened Western Pacific by entering into a pact providing her with military defenses."[5]

At the same time that MacArthur was making such pacifistic suggestions regarding the homeland of Japan, he was continuing to assert that the United States should retain military predominance in the Pacific. For this purpose the United States should annex the Ryukyus, especially Okinawa, and maintain bases there, in addition to annexing the islands which the Japanese had previously held as mandates.

[2] MacArthur occasionally expressed a certain *mystique* of free enterprise; for example, he felt that there would be no problem of prohibiting Japanese trade with Communist China, because a socialized China would be too unproductive to export anything.
[3] *Ibid.*   [4] *Ibid.*   [5] *New York Times*, November 5, 1949, 5:2.

MacArthur's suggestions for an early treaty were a source of embarrassment both to officials in the State Department, who feared the political consequences of releasing Japan in an enfeebled economic state, and also to the War and Navy Departments, which were interested in bases in Japan proper. Later, however, when the State Department began to recommend a generous treaty, it found MacArthur to be a useful ally, for even though their diagnoses of the political reform of Japan were radically different, they did agree on the importance of a generous treaty.

(2) *The War and Navy Departments.* In many ways the opinions of the War and Navy Departments were at the opposite pole from those of MacArthur.[6] Both departments were concerned about the indefensible position of Japan following a peace treaty and were therefore vigorously opposed to a quick treaty. They were skeptical of the ability of the United Nations to fill a power vacuum, and Secretary of the Navy Forrestal said frankly that "the United Nations was oversold."[7] Neither department was impressed by the anti-war clause of the Japanese Constitution, and hence both were willing to rebuild Japan's army if it would be useful as a defense against the USSR. Most of all, they were unwilling to give up Japan as a base for American forces. The Navy widely circulated a memorandum asking for a base at Yokosuka and airfields to protect it, and the Army wanted not only specific bases but free movement over the whole of the islands.

Even before the end of the war, it had been assumed that the United States would have major responsibility for security in the Pacific, and the Navy was most insistent on gaining control of the Japanese mandated islands and the Ryukyus. In order to have free use of these territories for military purposes, the War and Navy Departments wanted them assigned to the

[6] That MacArthur could publicly express opinions contrary to those of his superiors in the chain of command indicates, incidentally, how great his authority was.
[7] *Forrestal Diaries*, p. 266.

United States as "strategic trusteeships," rather than as ordinary trusteeships which would be subject to United Nations supervision. Legalistic maneuvering over the islands began as early as 1945 when Stimson, who was then Secretary of War, suggested that the islands were not properly to be called "colonies," but were "defense posts," and therefore it was appropriate to settle their status in Four-Power conferences rather than in a general trusteeship meeting.[8] We shall find that the military departments continued to suggest quasi-legal devices (e.g., a "half-treaty" with Japan) in order to retain positions which they considered necessary for security.

The military departments were not particularly concerned with most of the reforms introduced by MacArthur and therefore, to the extent that they considered such matters at all, were willing to reverse some of them in the interests of security. Forrestal, for example, consistently attacked the de-Zaibatsu policy as depriving Japanese industry of its best managers, thereby preventing the economic revival of the country.[9]

(3) *The Borton Group.* Opinion in the State Department concerning a treaty with Japan was not homogeneous, for there were different groups either directly concerned with the question or concerned with it in the context of other planning, and these had different perspectives on Japan. One of the most important points of view was that the defeated enemy Japan was capable of military revival and renewed aggression in the Pacific and Asia, unless appropriate preventive measures were taken. This point of view was the natural residuum of a bitter war, and it found expression in the Initial Post-Surrender Policy Directive for Japan (a product of the State-War-Navy-Coordinating Committee in 1945[10]), which asserted that the

[8] Henry L. Stimson and McGeorge Bundy, *On Active Service in Peace and War*, New York, Harper, 1948, p. 600.
[9] *Forrestal Diaries*, p. 328.
[10] For previous discussion of the work of this committee, see pp. 33ff. above.

PEACE PROPOSALS: 1947-1950

ultimate objective of the Allies in Japan was to guarantee that Japan would never again menace the peace. This document was noteworthy for the rigor of its anti-militaristic provisions and the fact that even the generous clauses—such as the encouragement of fundamental liberties and the proposal to allow the Japanese an adequate peacetime economy—were directed at the ultimate aim of security against Japanese militarism. It is not surprising that such ideas had considerable momentum, and that in spite of the outbreak of the Cold War there were numerous planners who thought of security in the Pacific primarily in terms of security against Japan.

A group headed by Hugh Borton, Special Assistant to the Director of the Office of Far Eastern Affairs, was entrusted with the early work of preparing drafts of a peace treaty with Japan. In an address to the Academy of Political Science in New York in November 1947, Dr. Borton reviewed the provisions of the Potsdam Agreement and the Initial Post-Surrender Policy Directive.[11] The address acknowledged the difficulties in sustaining a peacetime economy in Japan and approved highly of measures adopted by SCAP and the Far Eastern Commission for stimulating the Japanese textile industry and encouraging trade. A novel proposal of the address was that reparations be quickly settled, for this would eliminate doubt and thereby have a salutary effect on the Japanese economy—a proposal which was clearly consistent with Dr. Borton's general point of view. There was a reference to the Soviet refusal to attend the meeting of the Far Eastern Commission nations that the United States had proposed on July 11, 1947, for the purpose of discussing a peace treaty with Japan, but the only inference which he drew from this refusal was that a voting procedure would have to be worked out which would be acceptable to all the nations concerned.

The treaty draft drawn up by the Borton group in March 1947, and the revised drafts of August 1947 and January 1948,

[11] DSB, xvii, No. 438 (November 23, 1947), pp. 1001-5.

reflected the general idea that all precautions must be taken against a Japanese military renaissance. The Japanese were to be permitted no military forces other than internal police and a coast guard; no research of a primarily military nature, including research dealing with fissionable materials; no manufacture or operation of either military or civil aircraft; and no stockpiling of strategic raw materials in excess of normal requirements for current consumption. These restrictions were to remain in force twenty-five years after the establishment of peace unless the governments represented on the Commission of Inspection should otherwise decide. There was to be a Council of Ambassadors (representing the eleven nations at that time belonging to the Far Eastern Commission), which was to enforce these restrictive provisions, and a Commission of Inspection reporting to the Council of Ambassadors concerning any infractions of the demilitarization provisions. Japan was committed, furthermore, to ensure all the rights and freedoms of political democracy and to continue the economic reforms begun under the Occupation. Certain groups associated with militaristic activity were to be debarred from public office. The Council of Ambassadors was to be empowered to enforce both the economic reforms and the limitations on office-holding. Stringent reparations were to be imposed, and furthermore Japan was to accept the obligation to repay the United States for some of the dollar advances furnished during the Occupation. There were no provisions for the post-treaty security of Japan, and no grants of bases or other military advantages to the United States. In general, the conception of the world situation mirrored in the draft was that of World War II and not of the Cold War.

(4) *The Policy Planning Staff.* Since the Cold War was an undeniable fact in 1947, it was natural that many of the officials of the State Department began to see the problems of a retaliatory policy toward any particular nation, such as Japan, in the perspective of the Soviet threat. This was true in par-

ticular of the Policy Planning Staff, which was formed in April of 1947 especially in order to centralize the policy planning of the State Department. The head of it was George Kennan, a diplomat with long experience in the Soviet Union and one of the chief architects of the Containment Policy. This group raised the question whether the existing drafts for a treaty with Japan had not been written in a policy vacuum, or perhaps in the context of a pre-Cold War policy. Furthermore, they suggested that the technical details of the existing drafts would obscure the main point of the treaty and would not be looked at seriously. Most of all, they were skeptical about the advisability of writing into the treaty restrictions on sovereignty, such as commitments on the part of Japan to maintain various reforms instituted under the Occupation and to accept economic and military controls. A peace treaty, they felt, should return sovereignty and not restrict it, for attempts at restrictions would not endure and would cause resentment.

Members of the Planning Staff were doubtful about attempts to hasten a treaty with Japan. They regarded Japan's social, economic, and political situation as too unstable as yet to cast that nation loose in the hard world. The Occupation reforms, they felt, had weakened the prewar fabric of Japanese society. The reforms themselves were not objected to so much as the pace at which they had been enforced. The "purge" of 180,000 professional army officers, 30,000 imperial police officers, 10,000 imperial teachers, and most of the high bureaucracy appeared to them to have deprived the nation of the class which previously had provided leadership and carried responsibility, and there was no group ready to take its place. There was a possibility that after a treaty there would be a strong nationalist upsurge which would restore the old ruling clique, because there had not been time for Japan to absorb the reforms initiated by MacArthur. On the other hand, there was also a possibility that Communists in Japan, who had been released from the prisons at the beginning of the Occupation and allowed to operate freely, would take advantage of the disorganization of the country. Nor would the weak, decentralized police permitted by the Occupation authorities be sufficient to cope with internal disturbances and subversion. It was unrealistic to expect that a quickly released Japan would be friendly to the United States, since either an extreme reactionary or an extreme radical regime was very likely, and either would be hostile, and especially since the most pro-American among the Japanese, the conservative businessmen, had been among those purged.

Members of the Policy Planning Staff also felt that the economic prospects of Japan, with her industries crippled and still further to be weakened by reparations and with post-treaty restrictions on production and trade, were very dismal. They foresaw an economic collapse, with resulting misery which the United States could not allow for humanitarian reasons and which would also be an invitation to communism.

In short, their most urgent recommendations were that the United States should not push ahead immediately with a peace treaty, that it should use an extended Occupation period to clear up many problems which otherwise would have to be dealt with in a treaty, and that Japan should be strengthened economically and politically so that when released she would be stable.

Post-treaty security considerations were to be delayed along with the treaty itself. It was recommended that a security treaty should be negotiated only after signing and ratifying the general peace treaty, for linkage of the two would leave the United States open to the charge of dictation to the Japanese. The Staff was skeptical of predictions (by MacArthur, later echoed by Dulles) that Japan would feel bound to the United States because of the ideological reformation achieved by the Occupation. They did feel, however, that self-interest in the face of a traditionally hostile and still expansionistic Russia would naturally induce the Japanese to seek shelter in the Western alliance. The greatest threat, they felt, would not be an external military threat but the danger of Communist subversion; and to this there was no better countermeasure than rebuilding the country's economy and social and political system. Thus the Policy Planning Staff extended to Japan, *mutatis mutandis*, much of the logic of the European Recovery Program.

It is not known when in 1947 these ideas on Japan were broached in the Policy Planning Staff. A plausible guess, however, is that a systematic consideration of the future of Japan took place in the late fall or early winter of 1947. Doubtless the ideas which crystallized at that time had spread beyond the Policy Planning Staff in the State Department sometime earlier, especially since they were largely corollaries of the Containment Policy. One may even find intimations of these ideas in Acheson's speech in Cleveland, Mississippi, on May 8, 1947, in which he described Japan and Germany as "two of the greatest workshops of Europe and Asia" which must be reconstructed as soon as possible.

Activity and Stalemate on the Treaty

The foregoing survey indicates that in 1947 there was not sufficient consensus among the various agencies of the United States government to warrant immediate participation in a peace conference for Japan. There was, however, great pressure in favor of concluding a treaty very quickly. Much of this pressure came from economy-minded Congressmen and citizens. It was said that the Occupation of Japan was costing a million dollars per day, and actually the apportioned aid, even apart from army expenses, was nearly this great: 108 million in 1945-1946, 294 million in 1946-1947, 357 million in 1947-1948.[12] When the War Department requested 725 million dollars for relief in Germany, Japan, and Korea, Representative

[12] Robert A. Fearey, *The Occupation of Japan: Second Phase, 1948-50*, New York, Macmillan, 1950, p. 218.

PEACE PROPOSALS: 1947-1950

John Taber, the Chairman of the House Appropriations Committee, was hesitant and requested the advice of Herbert Hoover. Hoover recommended immediate peace treaties with both Japan and Germany, on the ground that these countries would then be able to participate in the capitalistic economy of the world, which would render them self-sufficient and no longer dependent on United States aid. It was probably quite unrealistic to believe that the conclusion of a peace treaty, even of one which did not impose economic penalties, would solve Japan's economic difficulties at that time. Hoover's argument was nevertheless widely accepted in Congress, and in May a resolution was offered in the House of Representatives by Congressman Poulson of California recommending that a treaty with Japan be negotiated immediately.

MacArthur also exerted pressure on the State Department to hasten a peace conference. He felt that the main work of the Occupation had been completed, that the reforms initiated had taken root, and that his role in a prolonged occupation would merely be that of a guardian, a role which was not to his taste.[13] Whatever his motivations, MacArthur succeeded in focusing attention on the question of a peace treaty with Japan by announcing his views to a gathering of foreign correspondents in Tokyo on March 17, 1947. His position, which we have summarized previously, was at odds with the views of the military departments and of various agencies of the State Department, particularly in regard to the timing of the treaty and to post-treaty security. What most displeased the authorities in Washington, however, was the fact that MacArthur's surprising announcement, which could not fail to appeal both to large segments of Congress and to many of the Japanese themselves, seemed to be an attempt to force their hands prematurely.[14]

---

[13] E. J. Lewe van Aduard, *Japan from Surrender to Peace*, New York, Praeger, 1954, p. 62.

[14] This was a technique that seemed to be employed at various

PEACE PROPOSALS: 1947-1950

Perhaps as a consequence of MacArthur's press conference, perhaps independently, there was active planning in the State Department during the spring of 1947 concerning the future of Japan. The deadlock over Germany in the fourth plenary session of the Council of Foreign Ministers in Moscow in March and April indicated that there was little to gain by referring the questions of peace with Japan to that body. Suggestions were made in the State Department that a practical alternative to the Council might be a body representing the eleven nations of the Far Eastern Commission, most of which were sufficiently closely attached to the incipient Western alliance to guarantee a two-thirds or better vote against the Soviet Union on crucial security matters. These suggestions were reenforced by statements in May of Foreign Secretary Bevin of Great Britain, who had been urged by some of the Commonwealth nations to secure for them a voice in the Japanese settlement. The result of this new line of thinking was an invitation by the United States on July 11, 1947, to the ten other members of the Far Eastern Commission to a preliminary conference of deputies and experts, for the purpose of preparing a draft of a treaty with Japan.[15] Stress was placed on the expediency of the same broad representation of the victors as had been established for the Far Eastern Commission; but it was also suggested that any possibility of veto by a single power be eliminated by fixing a two-thirds majority as the rule for decision. When the draft was far enough advanced, a general conference of all the states at war with Japan would be convened. The tentative date suggested was August 19, 1947.

The proposed conference did not materialize, for reasons which were in varying degrees predictable. The Soviet Union was fully aware of its disadvantageous position at such a conference and objected, claiming that the Potsdam protocol

---

times by MacArthur, particularly during the Korean War, and that finally culminated in his removal by Truman for insubordination.

[15] DSB, xvii, No. 421 (July 27, 1947), p. 182.

made the Council of Foreign Ministers the mandatory body for preparation of a treaty with either Germany or Japan. Great Britain and the Commonwealth countries declined to send representatives by the date proposed, because it conflicted with a Commonwealth conference scheduled for August 26 in Canberra. The date of the Canberra Conference had been set before the American invitation was issued, and since objectives in Japan were an important part of the agenda, it was felt that a ministerial discussion of policy should precede the instruction of delegates to a meeting of all the Far Eastern Commission powers. Finally, objections were raised by China to the mode of voting. China first proposed that negative votes by any two of the Big Four (United States, Great Britain, USSR, China) would constitute a veto, and then later, in September, unexpectedly changed its proposal and agreed with the USSR that a negative vote by a single one of these powers would be a veto. The motivation for this switch was probably fear that Chinese participation in a peace conference from which the Soviet Union abstained would be construed by the latter as a violation of the Sino-Soviet agreement of 1945, which forbade a separate peace with Japan, and the Soviet Union would then have a legal excuse for aiding the Chinese Communists.

It is somewhat puzzling why the American invitation to the FEC nations took the form it did, since it was easily foreseeable that the proposed procedure and date would be repugnant to the USSR and to the Commonwealth respectively. If the intention had been to abandon hope of Russian participation, as the State Department was definitely envisaging by 1949 and as actually happened in the final peace settlement, it still is not clear why the conflicting date of the Commonwealth conference should have been ignored. One possibility is that the State Department had strong premonitions that the Canberra Conference would stiffen Commonwealth support of a punitive Japanese treaty and hoped that an earlier meeting of all the

PEACE PROPOSALS: 1947-1950

Far Eastern Commission powers would endorse American ideas for a mild treaty which took primary account of security against the USSR. Some of the observers from Australia and New Zealand, in particular, entertained such a suspicion.[16] This view is not convincing, however, because it does not take account of the heterogeneity of opinion among the American authorities, which had not been resolved at the highest level by the time of the invitation. Indeed, as late as June 19, 1947—less than a month before the invitation—the FEC had adopted, with the concurrence of the American representative, its Basic Post-Surrender Policy for Japan, which was highly punitive and restrictive, and was in fact largely adapted from the Initial Post-Surrender Policy Directive of 1945. It is possible that if the choice of a conflicting date was intentional and not merely a clumsy coincidence, the reason was a desire of the State Department to delay a settlement in Japan. There were, as we have seen, strong elements in the State Department that thought this desirable, and surely others not particularly sympathetic with delay of the treaty may nevertheless have thought it desirable to have time to settle the interdepartmental differences of opinion. The invitation to the FEC nations could be cited as evidence to Congress and the public that steps were being taken toward peace with Japan, while the non-cooperation of the USSR, China, and the Commonwealth nations could be cited as reasons for not completing the project. If any Machiavellianism at all is to be imputed to the State Department at this time, it should perhaps be nothing more than the minor Machiavellianism of thinking up a device for gaining time.

The Canberra Conference deserves detailed attention, for it exhibited the unity of the Commonwealth in favoring a restrictive treaty with Japan, an attitude which to a large degree persisted until the final settlement at San Francisco in

[16] See, for example, W. Macmahon Ball, *Japan, Enemy or Ally?*, New York, John Day, 1949, p. 91.

PEACE PROPOSALS: 1947-1950

1951. One of its primary purposes was to strengthen the influence of the Commonwealth in general, and of Australia and New Zealand in particular, in any future peace conference regarding Japan. These nations did not share MacArthur's optimism concerning the conversion of the Japanese to pacifism and democracy. During the war they had been threatened by invasion, and Australia had actually experienced some Japanese bombing. It was natural, therefore, that they should fear a resurgent Japan and minimize the danger of remote Russia. They also had some fear of ruinous commercial competition from an unchecked Japanese industrial recovery, though it was the United Kingdom which was most apprehensive on this score. Although the Australian Minister of External Affairs, Evatt, insisted in Tokyo on July 24, 1947, that the Canberra Conference was not intended as a conspiracy against American policy, the fact remained that the Commonwealth countries were concerned about the trend in American policy away from economic and political controls in Japan.

It was not surprising, therefore, that when the Canberra Conference adjourned on September 2, its final communiqué should have been little more than a confirmation of the severe terms of the Potsdam Declaration and the FEC's Basic Post-Surrender Policy. The communiqué pointed out that "Although in accordance with practice at such Conferences, no formal decisions were taken, the discussions revealed a wide harmony of views among the nations of the British Commonwealth represented at the Conference." It then went on to assert that the discussions also "made it appear that a close correspondence exists between the various views expressed at Canberra and those of the United States of America, as well as of the other powers primarily interested in the settlement." As the next paragraph shows, however, these American views were those that had found expression in the Potsdam Declaration and the post-surrender policy declarations, not the more recent ideas shaping themselves around the new desire to build Japan into an effective ally against Soviet expansion.[17]

It is easy to understand the fears on the score of both physical and economic security which prompted the British countries in this reaffirmation of the principle of a severely restrictive treaty. In the light of the experience with Germany from 1918 to 1939, it is not so clear how the delegations at Canberra thought it possible to reconcile so many repressions with their declared desire for "a democratic and lasting peace settlement" that would assist in bringing about "a democratic, peace-loving Japan." The laconic communiqué offers no solution of this conundrum.

[17] The tone and substance of the discussions are adequately summed up in three paragraphs:

"Security against future aggression by Japan was a major concern of the Conference throughout all its discussion on all subjects. Delegates noted with satisfaction that General MacArthur and the forces under his command had already virtually completed the disarmament and demilitarization of Japan. The Conference therefore directed particular attention to ensuring that Japan would not be in a position to rearm or to recreate dangerous war potential. There was general acceptance of the view that encouragement should be given to the positive measures designed to bring about a democratic, peace-loving Japan which would have neither desire nor ability to menace other nations.

"With regard to political provisions, the removal from office of militarists and dissolution of ultra-nationalistic societies was approved, and the opinion was expressed that steps should be taken to prevent their return. The peace treaty should provide for recognition and enforcement of fundamental human rights and freedom of association. The delegates paid particular attention to the development and protection of trade unions as an essential element in encouraging democracy in Japan. Delegates noted with approval the principles underlying the new Japanese Constitution.

"With regard to economic and financial provisions, it was felt that key war industries such as armament and aircraft manufacture and the production of strategic materials of an uneconomic character should be prohibited. Production and capacity in key industries which could form part of war potential should be limited to defined levels. These restrictions in the interests of security should be supplemented by control of Japanese imports. Any restrictions imposed on the Japanese economy should not go beyond what is demanded by considerations of military security." ("Japanese Peace Settlement," New Zealand Department of External Affairs, Publication No. 38, Wellington, N.Z., 1947, pp. 4-6.)

PEACE PROPOSALS: 1947-1950

The negative results of the July invitation to the FEC nations did not put an end either to the clamor for a peace treaty or to overt activity to achieve one. In the latter part of 1947 and throughout 1948 pressure of various sorts was brought to bear on the United States government in favor of an early peace settlement. Thus, on August 16, the *New York Times* carried an editorial advocating an early peace with or without the Soviet Union, and it is probable that this idea already had strong support in government circles. "No agreement and no moral law," the *Times* wrote, "requires us to perpetuate a situation which costs us hundreds of millions of dollars yearly and imperils the welfare of the whole Far East." On September 25 Senator Taft called for a treaty with Japan "as rapidly as possible," as part of a seven-point foreign policy program. On November 21 a subcommittee of the Armed Services Committee of the House of Representatives recommended a speedy settlement, regardless of Russian abstention or participation, and specifically criticized the great cost of continuing the Occupation. There was also external pressure. For example, on November 3, 1948, the General Assembly of the United Nations unanimously approved a resolution introduced by Mexico urging the Great Powers to compose their differences and make treaties with both Germany and Japan.

One of the lines of action of the Department of State during this period was an attempt to overcome the resistance of China and the USSR to the voting procedure originally proposed by the United States for the peace conference. In October of 1947 Acting Secretary of State Lovett was still optimistic that negotiations would begin by the end of the year, and he appointed Maxwell Hamilton as the Deputy of the Secretary of State in the prospective negotiations. However, the refusal of China and the Soviet Union, in January 1948, to change their position on the veto caused an indefinite delay of the proposed conference.

PEACE PROPOSALS: 1947-1950

In the meanwhile, work continued on various drafts for the treaty. One was ready in August 1947 that presumably would have been presented to the conference of FEC powers, had it convened at the time originally suggested by the United States; and another draft was completed in January 1948. It is noteworthy that both these drafts were restrictive and punitive.[18] There were no indications of devices which would have bound Japan to the Western alliance, and indeed, the drafts have altogether a pre-Cold War flavor. It is not surprising, therefore, that despite the great labor involved in preparing them, they were in the long run discreetly abandoned. The overt activity of planning conferences and preparing drafts was much less significant for the final peace settlement with Japan than work which was proceeding elsewhere and which will be described in the following sections.

New Policies of the Occupation

During 1947 and 1948 the economic policies of the Occupation authorities in Japan underwent radical changes—not dramatically promulgated, not initiated from a single source, yet all tending in a definite direction.

The proposals and measures on economic matters early in the Occupation had several aims: to provide compensation to Japan's wartime victims in the form of reparations and commercial protection, to strip Japan of industrial equipment which might be used for military purposes, and to reconstitute the structure of the society so as to eradicate the spirit of militaristic adventuring. By the end of 1947 these proposals had been partly, but only partly, fulfilled. Heavy industry had virtually halted, in accordance with the recommendations of the Pauley Commission. Some machine tools had been sent as reparations to China, the Philippines, Great Britain, and the Netherlands, but most of the equipment originally earmarked

---

[18] See the discussion of the Borton group, pp. 58-59.

for reparations had not been shipped. The Diet had passed land reform legislation, as required by SCAP, and as a result there was a considerable increase in the number of small landholders, but unfortunately also a decrease in agricultural productivity. The right of labor to organize and bargain collectively was granted by the Diet at the end of 1945, and the labor movement developed rapidly, with 5 million workers organized by the beginning of 1947; *prima facie* this was perhaps the most complete success of any of the economic reforms of the Occupation, although the threat of a general strike against the Yoshida government (which a SCAP decree prevented) dampened the enthusiasm of the Occupation authorities about this particular reform. The anti-Zaibatsu program was formally, at least, pursued with great vigor. A Holding Company Liquidation Commission was formed in November 1945, for the purpose of disposing of the Zaibatsu holdings, and several pieces of legislation were passed by the Diet which aimed at permanent decentralization of the Japanese industrial and commercial systems. Various circumstances, however, made the accomplishments of this program dubious: e.g., the fact that various officials of the Liquidation Commission, including the chairman, had been associated with the Zaibatsu; the notoriously loose auditing system then current in Japan; and the strong family ties which enabled purged businessmen to direct their enterprises at a distance.[19] The FEC adopted a detailed and far-reaching plan on decentralization of the Japanese economy (FEC-230) in May of 1947 that might very well have led to the accomplishment of the anti-Zaibatsu program, but the change of economic policy occurred before this plan was put into effect.[20] In general the policy innovations constituted a trend toward relaxation of restrictions on Japanese industry and trade, and away from many of the social and economic reforms.

[19] Ball, *op.cit.*, pp. 125-28.
[20] Fearey, *op.cit.*, pp. 65-66.

PEACE PROPOSALS: 1947-1950

The primary reason for these innovations was the realization of the disintegrated state of the Japanese economy, together with the corollary that the United States would have to bear the expense of maintaining a marginal standard of living in Japan. MacArthur's press conference of March 17, 1947, acknowledged the economic crisis and suggested that Japan be allowed to resume trade in order to obtain the means for importing food. The speech by Acheson on May 8, 1947, mentioned above, similarly referred to the devastation of Europe and Asia and stated that recovery depended partly upon the reconstruction of the economy of Japan, which he characterized as the workshop of Asia. It is not surprising, therefore, to find that the FEC not only made great efforts to stimulate the Japanese cotton industry, but even permitted, after January of 1948, the revival of the iron and steel industry.

Various commissions suggested relief and aid to the Japanese economy as well as proffering advice on financial difficulties. Thus, in July 1947, a commission under the chairmanship of Clifford Strike recommended a drastic scaling-down of the reparations program proposed by the Pauley Commission. The conclusion of Strike's report is significant both as an indication of the trend and as a statement of motivations: "Removal of productive facilities (except primary war facilities) which can be effectively used in Japan would hurt world production; would reduce the likelihood of her becoming self-supporting, and in any case increase the time required for accomplishing this objective; would be expensive to the American taxpayer; and, in our opinion, would not be in the best interests of the claimant nations."[21]

In March 1948, Under Secretary of the Army William Draper visited Japan, accompanied by a group of eminent American businessmen under the chairmanship of Percy Johnson, and recommended an end to reparations, economic

[21] Quoted in Ball, *op.cit.*, p. 169.

PEACE PROPOSALS: 1947-1950

assistance above relief in order to rebuild Japan's industry, and an increase of Japan's merchant marine. The Johnson report was influential in securing an appropriation in May 1948 of 150 million dollars for economic rehabilitation in Japan. In June a report was submitted by a mission headed by Ralph Young of the Federal Reserve Board, calling for a strong economic stabilization program, including price and wage controls, control over allocation of raw materials, stricter tax collections, and a fixed exchange rate for the yen. These recommendations, unfortunately, were not put into effect by the government of Premier Ashida nor by his successor Yoshida, and MacArthur was forced to impose on the Yoshida government a nine-point economic stabilization program in order to check inflation, profiteering, and industrial slackness. It should be remarked that the intervention of SCAP at this point was by no means inconsistent with the trend toward generosity in economic matters, for this instance of severity was as much directed toward the economic revival of the country as were the grants of aid.

It is of interest to note the extent of Japan's economic progress under the new program. In 1948 Japan's imports totaled $683 million, and her exports $258 million; in 1949 her imports totaled $901 million, and her exports $511 million.[22] In other words, about 37 per cent of imports were balanced by exports in 1948, whereas approximately 60 per cent of imports were paid for by exports in the following year, after the economic reforms were instituted. This was a great improvement, but it still left a highly unfavorable balance of trade. It was not until the Korean War, when American expenditures in Japan were enormous, that Japan's economy attained a reasonably stable condition. Incidentally, the assistance rendered to the Japanese economy by the United States was such that one commentator was led to say that Japan treated the United States as an imperial country treats a colony—it takes raw

[22] Fearey, *op.cit.*, p. 218.

PEACE PROPOSALS: 1947-1950

materials from the colony, processes them, and then uses the colony as a market.

Economic rehabilitation was also the principal motivation for checking some of the reforms instituted by the Occupation. Thus, in January 1948, Secretary of the Army Kenneth C. Royall suggested that the decentralization program be reversed, in the interest of greater productivity. It was his feeling that since the men who had been the most active in developing and running Japan's war machine—military and industrial —were among the ablest and most successful leaders of the country, their services would in many instances contribute to its economic recovery. George Kennan visited Tokyo in February 1948, and in a series of conversations attempted to convince MacArthur that the extent and pace of the reforms had so weakened Japanese society that a sudden termination of the Occupation would be disastrous. In particular, he suggested that the purge of the conservative businessmen had been carried too far, for not only were these men indispensable in managing the country's economy, but they were ideologically more sympathetic to the United States than any other group.

Retreat on this (or on any) issue cannot have been an easy matter for a man of General MacArthur's temperament. However, the task of persuading MacArthur to reverse the policy of decentralizing the Japanese economy may have been expedited by the fact that SCAP had recently been accused of fostering socialism in Japan. MacArthur had evidently been stung by these accusations, and he had written a long letter to the Committee for Constitutional Government in New York defending the policies of the Occupation.[23] The implicit principle of MacArthur's regime had been to shape Japan in the image of America. Since the feudal family structure and monopolistic organization of the Zaibatsu were un-American,

[23] *Political Reorientation of Japan*, p. 778.

it had been natural for him to curb these combines. However, he had no intention of allowing the campaign against the Zaibatsu system (which he had characterized as "in effect a form of socialism in private hands"[24]) to become prelude to state socialism, a system equally un-American in his estimation. It is not known which of these influences was decisive in bringing about a reversal of SCAP's decentralization policy, but there is no doubt that by May 1948, when a Deconcentration Review Board was invited to Japan, such a reversal had taken place.[25] All but 30 of the 325 organizations listed to be investigated at the beginning of 1948 were dismissed without action,[26] and in December 1948 SCAP announced to the FEC that the deconcentration program had been essentially completed.[27] Thus, there was never an explicit announcement of the new policy, but appearances were preserved by proclaiming the success of the old one.

The relaxation of the anti-Zaibatsu program was paralleled by the imposition of controls on the labor unions. During the first half of 1948 there had been a series of strikes and demands for wage increases that disrupted production and threatened to aggravate the inflation of the currency. In July there was a threat of a strike of public service workers (a very large segment of Japanese labor, since the government operated many of the railroads and communications services, and held monopolies over tobacco and other products). SCAP forced the government, which was very reluctant, to revise the National Public Service Law so as to prohibit strikes of all public service workers. Other strikes—in the coal, electrical, and fiber industries, and in the private railways—were prevented by unofficial but firm warnings by the Occupation authorities. The repression of strikes, after the encouragement of unionism, was bitterly resented by Japanese labor, and one of the repercus-

[24] Ibid., p. 776.
[26] Ibid.
[25] Fearey, op.cit., p. 61.
[27] Ibid., pp. 65-66.

sions was a rapid growth of Communist influence in the labor movement during the first half of 1949, accompanied by sabotage, violence, and even assassination.[28] The Soviet representative on the FEC, meanwhile, opposed the revision of the National Public Service Law and the imposition of the nine-point economic stabilization plan and in general exploited the resentment against the new Occupation policies in order to gain favor for the USSR among the workers.

By the end of 1949 the leadership of the unions had generally been recovered by moderate elements, partly because of public revulsion against labor violence, partly because of a realization that the welfare of labor depended upon the economic recovery of the country as a whole, and partly because of the influence of SCAP.[29] Very likely, however, the evidence of Communist strength among the workers at this time vitiated much of the pressure, both among the Occupation authorities and in Washington, for a rapid peace settlement.

We have emphasized that the reversal of economic and social policies by the Occupation authorities in Japan was due primarily to the economic distress of Japan rather than to considerations of global strategy. Nevertheless, the innovations in Japan were consistent with American global strategy and certainly received some of their impetus from the architects of the Containment Policy. Part of the original conception of the Marshall Plan was the realization that economic chaos in a country provided an opportunity for Communist propaganda and infiltration, and, as we have seen, the Plan was approved by Congress largely on the ground that it would serve as an economic weapon against the expansion of communism. The same reasoning clearly applied to Japan. It is significant that the early proposal by Acheson to reconstruct the "workshop of Asia" was made in the context of a general sketch of aid programs, including the Marshall Plan and aid to the anti-Com-

[28] *Ibid.*, pp. 82-83.
[29] *Ibid.*, p. 84.

munist governments of Greece and Turkey.[30] Thus, although the immediate concern of the various technical missions sent to Japan in 1947 and 1948 was economic, and although the immediate purpose of SCAP's shift of policy with regard to the Zaibatsu and the unions was also economic rehabilitation, a definite political objective always hovered in the background.

A New Conception of the Peace Treaty

The events sketched in the previous section indicate that a new outlook on Japan was developing in many of the responsible agencies of the United States government. Step by step Japan was treated less as a defeated enemy and more as a potential member of the family of free nations. This conception was finally crystallized in November 1948, in a decision of the National Security Council. This decision has not been published, but some of its contents are known from later memoranda: Japan was to be strengthened economically and socially, so that after the termination of the Occupation it would be stable and—of its own initiative—friendly to the United States. As steps toward this end, SCAP was to shift responsibilities as rapidly as possible to the Japanese, and SCAP personnel would be reduced; a 150,000-man national police force was to be organized; Japan would be allowed to assimilate the reform programs at its own pace and in its own way; and the psychological impact of the Occupation on Japan would be reduced to a minimum. It may be observed that this decision to a large extent embodied the recommendations made by Kennan of the Policy Planning Staff a year earlier.

If any one event is to be designated as *the* turning point in America's postwar policy toward Japan, it should be this National Security Council decision, though, as we have seen, it is more accurate to acknowledge that the reversal of policy was a gradual process. In any case, thereafter a punitive peace with Japan received consideration only in the backwaters of the

[30] DSB, XVI, No. 411 (May 18, 1947), pp. 991-94.

government, remote from the crucial loci of decision.[31] The main line of planning for a peace treaty proceeded under the premises of the National Security Council decision, and the treaty which Dulles finally negotiated was only the culmination of this line of planning.

There were, however, a number of hurdles to be cleared before a peace treaty consistent with the National Security Council decision could be negotiated.

In the first place, it was essential that satisfactory internal conditions in Japan be achieved. We have seen that in 1948-1949 conditions were far from satisfactory, because of the economic crisis, labor difficulties, and government instability. Furthermore, there was resistance from various sides to recommendations of the National Security Council. For example, SCAP was very hesitant about increasing the Japanese police force and, as late as November 1949, one finds Acheson writing to MacArthur asking his cooperation in implementing this and others of the NSC recommendations.[32] It was not until July 1950, when American troops in Japan were being sent to Korea, that SCAP authorized a 75,000-man police force.

Secondly, it was necessary to reach a decision on a post-treaty security arrangement for Japan. There was considerable disagreement on this question within the United States government. The extent of this disagreement can be gauged by the

[31] That such backwaters existed is indicated by a new draft of the peace treaty in September 1949. This draft was not very different from the punitive draft of January 1948, which was mentioned earlier in the chapter. It *did not impose reparations, but it did contain re*strictions on the sovereignty of Japan and on the nation's war-making ability. The Japanese were not to engage in certain manufactures that could be put to military use, and troops (85 per cent of whom were to be American) were to remain in Japan for some time after the peace settlement.

[32] It should be noted that there were sound reasons for hesitating on the reconstitution of a strong civil police in Japan. The police had been used successfully by extremist groups in the decades before World War II to crush any opposition to their militaristic policies, and it was possible that they might again be used for the same purpose by a reviving reactionary movement.

PEACE PROPOSALS: 1947-1950

statements of Secretary of the Army Royall in Tokyo in February 1949, and by the consequent repercussions. Royall had visited United States army installations in Japan and was evidently not impressed by their strength or preparedness. He made unofficial statements at a press conference that Japan would be lost in case of war with the Soviet Union and, to prevent the American garrison from being sacrificed needlessly, it should be completely withdrawn from Japan. He was reported to have said that, according to a number of strategists in Washington, American forces were too small to hold the line against Soviet aggression in both Europe and the Far East, and that Western Europe should have priority in our defense system. The reaction to these statements among powerful segments of the American armed forces here and in Japan was so strong that it evidently had been a diplomatic mistake to discuss such a radical strategy publicly. Royall himself retracted his remarks within a few days and declared that American troops in Japan would fight if attacked. It was apparent that any serious consideration of abandoning Japan was at an end, for the suggestion does not recur in official releases or in declassified memoranda.

This does not mean, however, that disagreement as to the mode of defending Japan was at an end. Lt. General J. Lawton Collins, Vice Chief of Staff of the Army, for example, stated at the end of February 1949 that American forces in Japan should be greatly strengthened, especially in view of the military successes of the Chinese Communists on the mainland.[33] A few days later MacArthur, though agreeing that we should defend Japan in case of aggression, stated that the Occupation forces probably did not require reenforcement. In particular, he thought that the Communist victory in China posed no new threat to Japan, because the Chinese lacked resources for a large-scale amphibious operation. In case of actual Soviet invasion of Japan, he felt that the American troops could be

[33] *New York Times*, February 26, 1949, 1:4.

PEACE PROPOSALS: 1947-1950

quickly reenforced by a large Japanese volunteer army, and he complimented the Japanese infantryman on being "the most stubborn in the world." He thought, however, that an attack on Japan was most unlikely, and that Japan preferred the role of neutral to that of an active ally.[34]

There was also disagreement on the possibility of rearming Japan so that she could be prepared to defend herself. Many suggestions to this effect were made in the Defense Department. MacArthur, however, continued to oppose the rearmament of Japan and to uphold the Constitution which he himself had fostered. A further indication of the openness of the question of post-treaty security arrangements in Japan was the publication in Manila on November 4, 1949, of a report of MacArthur's suggestions regarding the treaty, in which three alternative schemes for defending Japan were mentioned: (1) entrance of Japan into the United Nations and a guarantee of her territorial integrity by that organization, (2) establishment of United States military bases in Japan as a long-term arrangement, and (3) protection of Japan by joint United States-Commonwealth forces.[35]

It was clear that important decisions on security matters were required before a peace conference could be held. However, the cardinal principle of protecting Japan against aggression, and in particular against Soviet aggression, was fully established by the end of 1949. It was embodied in the treaty draft of October 13, 1949, to be discussed below, and also in the important statement of policy by Secretary of State Acheson before the National Press Club on January 12, 1950, in which the defense perimeter of the United States was delineated as follows:

... What is the situation in regard to the military security of the Pacific area, and what is our policy in regard to it?

In the first place, the defeat and the disarmament of Japan has placed upon the United States the necessity of assuming the military

[34] *Ibid.*, March 2, 1949, 22:2.   [35] *Ibid.*, November 5, 1949, 5:2.

defense of Japan so long as that is required, both in the interest of our security and in the interests of the security of the entire Pacific area and, in all honor, in the interest of Japanese security. . . . I can assure you that there is no intention of any sort of abandoning or weakening the defenses of Japan and that whatever arrangements are to be made either through permanent settlement or otherwise, that defense must and shall be maintained.

This defensive perimeter runs along the Aleutians to Japan and then goes to the Ryukyus. We hold important defense positions in the Ryukyu Islands, and those we will continue to hold. . . .[86]

Another obstacle to a peace settlement along the lines envisaged by the National Security Council decision was the difficulty of obtaining the consensus of America's Cold War allies. This was a matter of greatest importance, for a rift with the Commonwealth and with the nations of Southeast Asia would endanger the American security program, thereby canceling any strategic gain which might be achieved by a favorable settlement in Japan. Furthermore, participation in the peace settlement with Japan was a point of pride with the nations of the Far Eastern Commission, which had been often overridden by SCAP in the administration of occupied Japan; this was understood by many of the officers of the State Department, who therefore advised that the objectives of the United States should be pursued with delicacy and diplomacy.

We have already discussed the suspicious attitudes of the Commonwealth countries—in particular, of Australia and New Zealand—as exhibited at the Canberra Conference in the summer of 1947. The shift of American policies during the occupation of Japan did nothing to dissipate these suspicions, and indeed confirmed them. The United States, during 1948 and 1949, had championed the revival of Japanese trade and industry, which could well result in the long run in serious commercial competition for the Commonwealth countries. Furthermore, in relaxing controls on the Zaibatsu and imposing restrictions on the labor unions, the United States had moved

[86] DSB, XXII, No. 551 (January 23, 1950), pp. 115-18.

into a position of adopting the conservative elements in Japan as its friends; and this was regarded as ominous, since these elements had been implicated in Japan's imperialism. Australia, which had a Labour government at the time, was particularly critical of American favoritism to the conservatives, partly because of fear of a revival of Japanese militarism and partly for reasons of ideology; and the Australian representative on the Far Eastern Commission had vigorously opposed the curbs on the unions imposed by SCAP. The Philippine people shared the fear of Japanese militarism, and furthermore were intent on getting reparations, as were China and India. Great Britain occupied a position intermediate between that of the United States and of the radically anti-Japanese members of the Commonwealth, as was to be expected in view of her cooperation with the United States in the Cold War in Europe.

In the middle of September 1949, a very important series of conversations was held in Washington between British Foreign Secretary Bevin and Secretary of State Acheson, and between Sir Esler Dening, the British Undersecretary for the Far East, and the Far East experts of the State Department. The British officials were sympathetic with the central concern of the United States, that of strengthening security arrangements against the USSR, and suggested that this might best be achieved by a bilateral pact between Japan and the United States yielding post-treaty bases to American military forces in return for protection of Japan. They also agreed that a liberal, non-punitive treaty would be essential for drawing Japan into the Western camp. However, the British felt that more attention should be paid to the requirements of the Commonwealth countries, both in regard to security against Japan and in regard to reparations and economic protection. Furthermore, Bevin and Dening prodded Acheson to hasten the treaty (as they in turn had been pressed by critics in Parliament and by the Commonwealth countries). They argued that the continued occupation of Japan would alienate public opinion there, that the money spent by the United States there would not buy Japanese allegiance, and that the refusal of Congress to make fresh appropriations—always a possibility—could be very deleterious to opinion in Japan as long as the Occupation continued.

Procedural problems were discussed, and it was agreed that the eleven powers represented on the Far Eastern Commission should be present at the initial peace conference, as the United States had proposed in the summer of 1947. However, Acheson wanted advance agreement between the United States and the Commonwealth countries prior to such a conference, so that the essential American requirements could be easily carried by a two-thirds vote, regardless of Soviet resistance. Bevin agreed to act as intermediary between the United States and the Commonwealth at a forthcoming meeting in Canberra in November 1949, and he requested a written statement of American requirements to be presented on that occasion. At the conclusion of the conversations Acheson held a press conference in which he stated that the two countries had agreed on the urgency of a peace treaty with Japan.[37]

In order to comply with Bevin's request, the Under Secretary's Office of the State Department was instructed on September 29 to prepare quickly a fresh treaty draft, and on October 3 Acheson wrote Secretary of Defense Johnson to provide a statement of minimum United States security and defense requirements and also to detail an officer to work with the State Department on matters of joint concern.

The new draft was ready on October 13, 1949. It is a document of very great interest, since it was the first Japanese treaty draft to be written with full awareness of the Cold War, the Containment Policy, and the National Security Council decision of November 1948. The underlying concept of the draft was the restoration of sovereignty with as few restrictions

[37] *New York Times*, September 15, 1949, 3:4.

as possible. The Far Eastern Commission, the Allied Council for Japan, and SCAP were to be abolished, and no control or inspection agency (such as the Council of Ambassadors contemplated in previous drafts) was to take their place. Japan was required to preserve a democratic government, including basic rights of free speech, freedom of religion, and so forth; but the agrarian, labor, and deconcentration reforms imposed by the Occupation were not specifically mentioned and were left to the discretion of the Japanese themselves. Japan remained obligated to make reparations, but there was no reference to the stock of gold in Japan and owned by Japan in neutral countries, thereby exempting Japan from making indemnification from this stock. As in the January 1948 draft, the obligation of Japan to repay all GAROIA and EROA grants from the United States had priority over all reparations, but the obvious intent of this clause (as explained by an accompanying commentary) was to give the United States control over the volume of reparations to be exacted by the other combatant nations.

Many technical matters were put into annexes, so that the main body of the treaty would not be cumbersome, yet loose ends would not be left which might give rise to disputes that would embitter post-treaty relations. The accompanying commentary stated explicitly the motivations and intentions implicit in the text of the draft. The primary motivation was to align Japan with the United States in world affairs. This objective could best be obtained if Japan was not put into a strait jacket of restrictions or humiliated by the terms of the treaty, and if the treaty was sufficiently generous so that the USSR and Communist China could not later undercut it by a more liberal offer. Insistence on the preservation of the Occupation reforms would be construed as a humiliating restriction, but the omission of reference to these reforms did not constitute a repudiation of them, and indeed economic pressure and other modes of persuasion could influence the

Japanese to retain them. The commentary anticipated the legal problem that would arise if the Soviet Union did not sign the treaty; in that case, the abolition of the Far Eastern Commission and the Allied Council for Japan could be construed as a violation of the Moscow Agreement of December 1945. However, it was suggested that if this issue should arise, it could be referred to the International Court of Justice, not only in hope of a decision in favor of the United States but in expectation that the Soviet Union would be willing to submit to the Court in the first instance.

The October 13 draft contained no security provisions, as these were to be inserted after collaboration with the Defense Department. The Defense Department, however, felt that no post-treaty security arrangement could be as advantageous militarily to the United States as the situation during the Occupation, and therefore it claimed that the treaty was premature. In the next section we shall examine the counter-proposals of the Defense Department, and the State-Defense difference of opinion which continued until Dulles was empowered to settle it. It is sufficient for the present to note that because no decision was reached in Washington on security provisions, it was not possible to provide Bevin with a complete statement of American demands in time for either the Canberra meeting in November 1949 or the conference of Commonwealth Foreign Ministers in Colombo in January 1950.

It should be noted that the conception and many of the crucial details of the October 13, 1949, draft were very similar to the treaty finally negotiated by Dulles and signed at San Francisco in 1951. The only important divergence between the two situations was that in 1951 the ground had been cleared for a security pact with Japan, whereas in 1949 the Far East Section of the State Department envisaged such a pact but did not have sufficient influence within the United States government to carry out its conceptions. It is therefore perhaps not accurate to refer to Dulles as "the architect of the Japanese peace treaty," as has often been done, but rather as the one who successfully negotiated and carried out, albeit with various improvisations and innovations, a previous blueprint.

It should also be noted at this point that the October 1949 draft was thoroughly realistic. It embodied a very clear hierarchy of values and objectives—with national security at the apex—and a clear program for pursuing these objectives. It represented, however, a pragmatic appraisal of a state of affairs which, from the standpoint of the United States, was less favorable than at the end of World War II and even less favorable than in 1947; for it tacitly acknowledged that China was in hostile hands, and therefore the focus of strategic planning in the Far East would have to be elsewhere.

Unsettled Questions

A complete statement of American objectives in Japan was still not available in May 1950, when a British Commonwealth Consultative Conference convened in London, although the State Department had earnestly wished to present it to earlier conferences. As we have seen, the delay was due to the opposition by strong elements of the United States military forces to the termination of the Occupation. The difference of view between the State Department and the Defense Department on this issue must now be examined in more detail, along with the question of a separate peace with Japan and the question of Japanese public opinion—matters which became inextricably intertwined with the problem of post-treaty security.

The issue between the State and Defense Departments arose from their difference in perspective and consequent difference in weighing the relevant factors.[38] To the Defense Department, military strength overshadowed all other con-

[38] For a discussion of the following position, see *New York Times*, May 12, 1950, 4:2.

PEACE PROPOSALS: 1947-1950

siderations. The Occupation provided the maximum opportunities for military utilization of Japan, for any part of the country could be used at will as a base, and there was no question of restriction to certain delimited areas, much less of total exclusion. Although some officers continued to raise the objection that troops in Japan would be vulnerable in case of war with the Soviet Union, the prevailing opinion was that such troops would be a military asset; in fact, it was argued that a military force poised on the far eastern frontier of the USSR would be a great deterrent against aggression in Europe, for the greatest of Russian phobias was a war on two fronts.[39] The Defense Department also professed to be concerned with the military consequences of a treaty to which the USSR was not a signatory, for then the USSR would still be technically at war with Japan and, in accordance with the Moscow Agreement, might legally be allowed to continue the Occupation. It is not known, however, how seriously this reasoning was intended, and how much it was simply a cover for the main concern of the Defense Department.

The State Department, though fully aware of the indispensability of military strength, insisted upon the importance of psychological considerations. It argued that the growing resentment of the Japanese people against a continued Occupation would counterbalance its military value and, indeed, if the Communist party within Japan should cleverly exploit this resentment, the strength of the Occupation forces would be undermined. Furthermore, the State Department felt that the continuation of the Occupation afforded only short-run security advantages, whereas the willing provision of bases after a treaty—which could be expected only if the Japanese felt no rancor against the United States—would benefit

---

[39] The cogency of this argument is dubious, since a war on two fronts for the USSR would equally be a war on two fronts for the United States, and presumably an equal liability to the latter. In other words, there is no strategic parallel to World War II, in which a war in the Far East meant for the Soviet Union an engagement with an additional enemy.

PEACE PROPOSALS: 1947-1950

American defense arrangements in the long run. It is understandable that the State Department should be so sensitive to considerations of ideology and opinion, for it had witnessed in China the erosion and eventual defeat of Chiang Kai-shek's regime by an enemy which initally was far weaker in manpower and armaments but which was careful to win popular support.

As an alternative to the State Department's proposal to restore full sovereignty to Japan, and as a step toward a compromise, the Under Secretary of the Army, Tracy Voorhees, suggested in March 1950 a "half-treaty." This would nominally restore sovereignty and would allow the Japanese to exercise authority in civil matters, but it would retain SCAP and the Occupation troops. Through SCAP, potential control of the regime in Japan would remain. This device would also solve the problem of the legal right of a non-signatory USSR to send troops to Japan; because SCAP still would be in existence and therefore could legally control the number of Soviet soldiers entering the country. It is difficult to see what this "half-treaty" would have accomplished. In particular, it is doubtful that the Japanese would have construed such a conditional and qualified grant of sovereignty as signifying the end of the Occupation. Indeed, such a treaty would in effect have made Japan an American puppet state, and this hardly would have helped in the campaign for men's minds in Japan. However, such was the authority of the Department of Defense that in the spring of 1950 the Office of Far Eastern Affairs considered accepting Voorhees' plan.

It should be pointed out that in the State-Defense issue General MacArthur was an ally of the State Department. MacArthur was in favor of restoring full sovereignty to the Japanese, and was opposed to making a grant of bases a precondition for the treaty. Indeed, he was skeptical of the advantages of bases in Japan, especially since he thought an overwhelming percentage of the Japanese people opposed them, and he preferred to employ Okinawa as the bastion of the Pacific. MacArthur's diagnosis, which underlay his prescription, was probably quite different from that of the State Department, for he remained very sanguine about the reform of the Japanese ethos and the consequent bonds of friendship with the United States. Nevertheless, his support on the nature of the treaty was very helpful to the State Department, particularly since he had such strong Congressional backing.

The possibility that the USSR would not sign a treaty which was designed largely to American specifications was understood as early as 1947, when the Soviet Union objected so violently to having all the Far Eastern Commission nations voting on a basis of a two-thirds majority at a peace conference. As time passed, and the Cold War was more and more reflected in our policy toward Japan, it became increasingly probable that the major objective of the United States would be security against the USSR, and it could hardly be expected that the USSR would sign a treaty embodying this principle. Consequently, some thought was given in the State Department to the consequences of concluding a separate peace with Japan. The legal justifications for doing this were somewhat shaky. It is true that at Potsdam no *written* agreement was made concerning Japan, and the State Department relied heavily on this fact.[40] The Russians had claimed that a verbal understanding had been reached, and the absence of a written agreement was due only to the fact that the Soviet Union was at peace with Japan and had to observe the proper forms. Nevertheless, the State Department continued to insist that the absence of a written agreement was crucial.

As a matter of fact, when Secretary of State Byrnes was urging at Potsdam that China be made a member of the Council of Foreign Ministers, he had argued that China's presence on the Council would be of considerable advantage when the time came to draft a peace treaty with Japan. The

[40] DSB, xvii, No. 425 (August 24, 1947), p. 395.

United States wanted to have China made a member in order to build up her prestige as an important power. Both Churchill and Stalin were at first opposed to this move but subsequently yielded to the American view. However, there was no written agreement at the time indicating that the United States would be willing to see the draft of the Japanese peace treaty turned over to the Council of Foreign Ministers. In fact, Secretary Byrnes changed his mind on the subject when he saw the growing divergencies of interest between the United States and Russia on the future role of Japan in the Pacific, and when he contemplated the slightness of the effort Russia made in bringing about the defeat of Japan.

The advancing course of the Cold War and the growing determination of the United States that Japan should be kept on the side of the Western nations made it increasingly clear that the Council of Foreign Ministers, with its unanimity principle, could not find a basis for agreement on a peace treaty for Japan. While the long drawn-out dispute was carried on at the level of a procedural difference of opinion, it really was part of a deep struggle for power in the Pacific.

Eventually the responsible officials of the State Department were willing to risk a peace treaty without the participation of the Soviet Union. The anticipated consequences of such a move did not seem too adverse. There would no doubt be an intensification of propaganda and of attempts to browbeat or subvert the Japanese government into refusing to go along with American policy. There might be a Soviet offer of an attractive alternative treaty, but the American proposals were sufficiently liberal so that it would be hard for the Soviet offer to undercut them. It was also speculated that the Soviet Union would put pressure on Communist China not to trade with Japan; but, as it turned out, any planning to counteract this was superfluous, for it was the United States which put pressure on Japan not to trade with Red China.

PEACE PROPOSALS: 1947-1950

Although Washington was ready by 1950 to accept a peace with Japan without the Soviet Union, there was by no means general acquiescence in this idea in other capitals. Of the Commonwealth countries, India and Australia were strongly opposed to a separate peace—India, because it was trying to pursue a neutralist course in international affairs; and Australia, because it feared the build-up of Japan that would result from a peace along strictly American lines. Great Britain was not particularly pleased with the possibility of a separate peace, but on the other hand it agreed that Japan should be aligned with the West and understood that any attempts to assure this might well lead to Soviet abstention from the peace settlement.

Another source of potential conflict with the Commonwealth was the problem of which Chinese government to seat at a peace table. The United States, Australia, and New Zealand continued to recognize the Nationalist government, now displaced to Formosa, while Great Britain and India recognized the Communist government. It was evident that the achievement of American ends in Japan without alienating these friendly but divergent countries would require great finesse and diplomacy.

As the Office of Far Eastern Affairs in the State Department foresaw, the long-range success of security arrangements in Japan was contingent largely on the consensus of the Japanese themselves. Japanese opinion, however, was complex and heterogeneous. From October 15, 1948, until December 7, 1954, the Prime Minister of Japan was Shigeru Yoshida, who was generally quite pro-American. In the elections of January 1949—the first after Yoshida assumed office—his party, the Democratic-Liberal Party, won an absolute majority in the Diet, 264 seats against 202 seats for all other parties.[41] This victory was based partly on Yoshida's personal appeal, partly on disgust with the corruption of the previous regime, partly

[41] Fearey, *op.cit.*, p. 109.

on a vague "traditionalism" supported by his party, and partly on economic considerations,[42] and therefore the large vote in Yoshida's favor did not necessarily demonstrate a popular endorsement of his views on relations between the United States and Japan.

In November 1949, Yoshida for the first time indicated to the Diet that Japan would accept a peace treaty. He said that his government took no stand on the possible concession of military bases to the United States after the conclusion of the treaty.[43] On January 24, 1950, he made a speech in the Diet which echoed MacArthur's address of New Year's Day, 1950, to the effect that the anti-war clause of the Constitution did not imply that Japan had forfeited the right to self-defense. This was interpreted by the opposition parties as hinting that Yoshida's government might be willing to concede bases, and he was immediately attacked on this ground. By May 1950, Yoshida was indicating that he was willing to accept a separate peace with the West and forgo Soviet participation.[44] On June 1, 1950, the Japanese government issued a formal paper stating that a *de facto* peace already existed and that a treaty would be negotiated with any Allied nation which wished one—in effect, a declaration of willingness to accept a separate peace.[45] This paper made the question of separate peace one of the central issues of the elections to Japan's upper legislative house, the House of Councilors, on June 4. The results of the election, however, were inconclusive: Yoshida's party lost in percentage of popular votes but gained seats; the Green Breeze Society, which generally supported the government, and the Communists lost seats, while the Socialists made substantial gains; furthermore, local issues were important and blurred the question of a separate peace.[46]

[42] *Ibid.*, pp. 108-9.
[43] *New York Times,* November 12, 1949, 1:2.
[44] *Ibid.*, May 9, 1950, 14:2.
[45] *Ibid.*, June 2, 1950, 5:2.
[46] Fearey, *op.cit.*, pp. 209-10, 213-14.

PEACE PROPOSALS: 1947-1950

The fact remains, however, that there was widespread popular disapproval of a separate peace and of the commitment of Japan to either side in the Cold War. A poll as early as November 21, 1949, indicated that only 20.5 per cent of those interviewed favored dependence on the United States for future security. In January the Peace Problem Council for Japan, consisting of eminent representatives from the universities and public life, affirmed that the Japanese people desired neutrality, disarmament, an overall peace, withdrawal of all foreign military forces from Japanese soil, and guarantees of inviolability by the United Nations[47]—a remarkable program which largely ignored the realities of world politics of the time. In March the president of Tokyo University announced his opposition to granting bases to the United States, and his position received very strong support in the press.[48] On April 26 all the opposition non-Communist parties formed a joint Foreign Policy Council which favored an overall peace and subsequent neutrality.[49] An advisor to Yoshida, Shirasu, admitted in May that popular opposition to American bases in Japan was much greater than six months earlier, though he himself felt that neutrality was unfeasible and dangerous.

In these expressions of opposition to American bases and alignment with the United States there was undoubtedly an emotional element, a feeling of indignity involved in surrendering sovereignty over particular pieces of territory for an indefinitely long time to the nation which had played the leading role in defeating Japan in World War II. However, there was also a large element of realistic anxiety and calculation. The Soviet Union was very close—indeed, one of the Russian-occupied islands was but a few miles from the tip of Hokkaido—and very powerful, and now the mainland of China was occupied by a Communist government which had proved to be very effective militarily. The United States, on the other

[47] Lewe van Aduard, *op.cit.*, p. 149.
[48] Fearey, *op.cit.*, p. 212.   [49] *Ibid.*

hand, had suffered a loss of reputation by backing the losing side in China. Was it to Japan's self-interest to alienate the powerful Communist bloc of states by making a separate treaty with the West, and would the United States be willing and able to defend Japan in case of a war? Furthermore, Japan had learned by experience how vulnerable she was to atomic weapons, and since the Soviet Union had constructed an atomic bomb by 1950, Japan feared that involvement in war would lead to a nuclear attack. Finally, economic penalties might result from a separate peace. China had long been one of Japan's major customers, and alignment with the West might very well imply the loss of the China trade. It was not certain that the West would offer her compensations in trading opportunities elsewhere, especially in view of the demands of British commercial interests. Considering all of these difficulties, it was obvious that the negotiations with Japan—if they were to have lasting value—would be extremely delicate, more so, perhaps, than the negotiations required to convince the Allies of the American point of view.

CHAPTER V

THE MISSION OF JOHN FOSTER DULLES

THE Truman administration consistently attempted to obtain Republican support for the major elements of its foreign policy. This was particularly the case after 1947, when it became clear that the Containment Policy would have to be extended over an indefinite number of years in order to be successful, and would involve unprecedented—and to many isolationist minds, outrageous—military and economic commitments in peacetime. Although some isolationism survived among the Republicans in Congress, on the whole the opposition party supported such crucial measures as the European Recovery Program, the Military Defense Assistance Program, and the ratification of the North Atlantic Treaty agreement.

A serious exception to bipartisanship in foreign affairs, however, was the China policy. The scathing criticisms, including prolonged Congressional investigations, of the management of affairs in China by the State Department came mainly (though by no means entirely) from Republicans, who claimed that they had not been consulted on Far Eastern affairs as they had been on European problems. The State Department yielded to a large extent to its critics, despite its sustained argument that the Nationalist government had lost the civil war because of its own vices rather than because of lack of support from the United States. It was felt, however, in the spring of 1950, that further gestures would be useful toward restoring bipartisanship and, in particular, that it would be valuable to have a Republican spokesman on matters of foreign policy in the higher echelons of the State Department. For this purpose John Foster Dulles was appointed on April 6, 1950, as Foreign Policy Adviser to the Secretary of State.

THE MISSION OF JOHN FOSTER DULLES

Dulles was an understandable choice for this position. He had had considerable experience in international affairs—as a member of the reparations commission at the Versailles Peace Conference, as a leading lawyer, as a senior adviser at the San Francisco Conference which established the United Nations, and as a member of American delegations to the United Nations. As one of Dewey's principal backers in the Republican National Convention of 1940 and in the Conventions and campaigns of 1944 and 1948, Dulles occupied a position of power in the Republican Party and was acknowledged as its "shadow" Secretary of State. Furthermore, he had been actively involved in the operation of bipartisanship in foreign affairs. During the 1944 presidential campaign, Secretary of State Hull was concerned that the proposal of an international order of states should not become a political issue, as had happened in 1920. Dewey sent Dulles to confer with Hull, and they reached general agreement that there should be Republican-Democratic cooperation in setting up the United Nations organization.[1] His later work on the United Nations, as well as his position on the staff of the American delegation at the Council of Foreign Ministers in London in 1945, was in part a result of this initial experiment in bipartisanship.

In 1949 Dulles served in the Senate for four months, appointed by Governor Dewey when Robert Wagner, Sr., resigned, and he continued to work in the same spirit. He joined forces with Senator Vandenberg in order to persuade a number of the Republican senators to vote in favor of ratifying the NATO agreement and the Military Defense Assistance Program (though he also supported a $125 million appropriation for Nationalist China, which was counter to the wishes of the Administration). Finally, in his credo on foreign policy, *War or Peace*, Dulles presented an eloquent theoretical exposition of bipartisanship:

[1] John Robinson Beal, *John Foster Dulles: A Biography*, New York, Harper, 1957, pp. 97-101.

THE MISSION OF JOHN FOSTER DULLES

The United States cannot successfully bring about a coalition for peace unless the two major parties cooperate on major policies. . . .

Bipartisanship is not easy to define, nor is it easy to produce. It requires the President to bring responsible members of the opposition party into the making of his foreign policies; and it requires these members of the opposition party to cooperate loyally to get support in the Congress and in the country for the policies that have been worked out together.[2]

There is no clear evidence available that at the time of Dulles' appointment as Foreign Policy Adviser there was any intention to assign to him the task of negotiating a treaty with Japan. It does seem that Dulles himself had some interest in this problem, for two days after his appointment he requested Assistant Secretary of State Butterworth to brief him on matters relating to the Japanese peace treaty. He is quoted as saying later to Secretary of State Acheson: "You'll never get anything done unless you select someone in whom you have confidence, give him a job to do, and then hold him to results. Look at the Japanese Peace Treaty—the department has been discussing it for four years without result. Why don't you give someone one year in which to get action, with the understanding that if he can't do it, he fails? Give him a target and enough authority to get there."[3] Whether this statement was intended or construed as a request, the fact remains that on May 18, 1950, Dulles was assigned to handle the treaty.

[2] John Foster Dulles, *War or Peace*, New York, Macmillan, 1953, p. 122. Dulles understood that it was a very delicate matter to strike a balance between bipartisanship in the formulation of policies and healthy criticism by the opposition party, which is essential to a two-party system. It is by no means clear that he was always able to maintain this balance himself. For example, in his senatorial campaign against Herbert Lehman in the fall of 1949, "He accused Lehman of accepting Communist support, and also argued that his own defeat, since he symbolized bipartisan support of a Democratic administration which opposed Communism, would permit the Communists to 'chalk up another victory in their struggle to get into office here.'" (Beal, *op.cit.*, p. 113.)

[3] *Ibid.*, p. 116.

THE MISSION OF JOHN FOSTER DULLES

On the same day President Truman told his press conference that the Japanese peace treaty was the responsibility of the Secretary of State, thus implying that the Secretary would have his support in any conflict with the Department of Defense regarding the peace settlement.

At least one factor—over and above the wish to employ a Republican on Far Eastern affairs—which may have counted in favor of Dulles' appointment to this task was his status as an ex-senator and his general good relations with the Senate, for eventually any treaty would have to be presented to the Senate for approval before ratification.

Dulles' Conception of a Settlement with Japan

As we have seen, the planning in the State Department concerning peace with Japan was very heterogeneous, and the various treaty drafts and memoranda which were produced embodied a considerable range of ideas. It was inevitable, therefore, that when Dulles studied the materials prepared in the State Department on Japan between 1945 and 1950, he found much with which he could not agree. However, we have also seen that by the end of 1948 a line of planning initially supported by Kennan and the Policy Planning Staff began to be dominant—a line which treated policy regarding Japan in the light of global problems, which insisted on a liberal settlement with Japan, and which hoped to draw Japan into the Western alliance, thereby strengthening that alliance against the USSR. This line of planning was extremely congenial to Dulles, and, as we shall see in his first memorandum on Japan, he incorporated it into his own thinking. Indeed, the conception of a treaty to be found in the October 13, 1949, draft and in later modifications of this draft is to a high degree consistent with two of Dulles' deepest convictions regarding the preservation of peace. The first conviction was that the imposition of harsh, retaliatory terms on a defeated enemy, out of fear that the enemy would become militarily powerful once again, was a self-destroying device, for the harshness of the terms would necessarily inspire the enemy with a desire for vengeance. The historical basis for this point of view was, of course, the Versailles Treaty, the intention of which had been to prevent Germany from ever again threatening the peace of Europe, but the effect of which was to stimulate the resurgence of German militarism. The lesson of Versailles, according to Dulles, was that justice, fair play, magnanimity, and humanity were the essential ingredients not only for a moral peace settlement, but also for one which in the long run would be safe and successful.[4] The second conviction was that in the post-World War II era the greatest threat to peace was the Communist movement, which—regardless of shifts of timing and temporary compromises—was dedicated to consummating the world revolution.[5]

It is interesting to examine the contents of Dulles' first memorandum on Japan, issued on June 6, 1950—less than three weeks after he was assigned the task of treaty-making—in order to compare it with its antecedents, to see Dulles' own contributions, and to understand the subsequent evolution of the treaty.

(1) The memorandum first discusses long-range objectives concerning Japan. The Japanese should be peaceful, should preserve fundamental human rights, and should cultivate self-respect by not depending on outside charity. Furthermore, Japan should be part of the free world and friendly to the United States and should set an example to the rest of Asia by thriving in the free world, thus contributing to a general will to resist communism.

(2) Next there is a survey of geographical, economic, political, ethical, military, and racial problems. Japan's geographical

[4] Broadcast of March 1, 1951, in DSB, XXIV, No. 610 (March 12, 1951), pp. 405-6.
[5] Dulles, *op.cit.*, pp. 5-16.

situation makes her susceptible to falling into the Communist orbit, and the West must take the initiative to prevent this from happening. Provision must be made to prevent Japan from being economically dependent on the Communist countries. There may be difficulties in making Japan's Constitution work, and perhaps an advisory commission might be created to help her on this problem (possibly with MacArthur as its head, on the invitation of Japan). It may be difficult to preserve human rights, fundamental freedoms, and individualism in Japan, because of a tendency to extreme conformity and convention in all aspects of Japanese life, and propaganda may be required to achieve the requisite cultural revolution. There is a danger of indirect aggression—i.e., subversion—in Japan, and a strong police force must be created to deal with such a contingency. Finally, the racial barrier which might prevent Japan from joining a Western alliance must be broken down. For this purpose, it would help to permit a limited amount of Japanese immigration into the United States; in addition, it might be possible to capitalize on the Japanese feeling of racial and social superiority to the Chinese, Koreans, and Russians, and to convince them that as part of the free world they would be in equal fellowship with a group which is superior to the members of the Communist world.

(3) The memorandum then deals briefly with intermediate steps, before the final security arrangements. A phased withdrawal of the Occupation is proposed, but not spelled out; and a police force is to be established immediately under SCAP supervision.

(4) Next the content of the treaty itself is briefly sketched. Provision is to be made for a progressive reduction of the military occupation. The reforms of the Occupation period are to be noted and preserved. There are to be no reparations or economic restrictions. Post-treaty control machinery in Japan is to be avoided, except perhaps in regard to methods

of mass destruction. Provision is to be made for Japanese application for admission into the United Nations.

(5) The memorandum suggests that independently of the treaty, but concurrently, a security agreement should be concluded. This should involve all the nations participating in the preliminary conference (which presumably could include the USSR, whose role in the security arrangements is not specified by Dulles). Note should be made of Article 9 of the Japanese Constitution, the clause which disavowed war, but this Article should not be contractually embodied in the security arrangement or in the treaty.

(6) Finally, the memorandum makes some suggestions regarding treaty procedure. Information on American views should first be sent to the non-Communist members of the Far Eastern Commission, and the position of the United States might be modified by meritorious suggestions of these countries. Such an exchange of ideas, however, should not be carried to the point of formal or complete agreement on the detailed treaty text. Then a preliminary conference should be called, consisting of delegates from all countries represented on the Far Eastern Commission, and in addition from Indonesia, Ceylon, South Korea, and Indochina; a Japanese representative would also be on hand. To solve the problem of the two Chinas, both the Nationalist and the Communist regimes would be invited to send delegates, and each would be given one vote in case of disagreement, but only one vote between them on any issue which they agreed upon. In the preliminary conference all procedural questions would be decided by a majority vote, while treaty terms would be settled by a two-thirds vote. The preliminary conference was to be held in the late summer or fall of 1950 in Hawaii. Thereafter, a plenary conference of all nations which had been at war with Japan would meet in Tokyo. The United States delegation at both conferences was to be bipartisan, with Presidential direction in case of difference of opinion; SCAP and the Pentagon were

to have advisory status, and General MacArthur was to have plenipotentiary status at the plenary conference.

Most of the ideas of Dulles' memorandum were expressed in the latter stages of State Department planning for Japan, as we have seen in the previous chapter. The advisory commission to help Japan run her constitutional machinery seems to have been Dulles' innovation, however, though it is somewhat reminiscent of the supervisory commissions envisaged in the treaty draft of January 1948, and earlier drafts. The recommendation to drop all reparations is in the spirit of the liberal draft of October 1949, but is yet more generous. The suggestion that the Japanese feeling of superiority to other Oriental nations be fostered and turned to our advantage seems to have originated with Dulles and is disconcerting; for, apart from its dubious morality, it indicates a rather narrow concentration on the settlement with Japan, while a truly global strategy would also involve alignment, and perhaps fellowship, with other Asiatic peoples. The suggestion that all the participants in the preliminary conference should be involved in security arrangements with Japan is an innovation and is *prima facie* inconsistent with the objective, stated at the beginning of the memorandum, that Japan was to be aligned with the United States; but undoubtedly what Dulles had in mind was a device whereby Japan's security would be formally guaranteed by a group of powers, including the USSR, even though the major responsibility as well as the major military advantage would belong to the United States.

Of the innovations expressed in this memorandum, perhaps the wisest was the suggestion to eliminate reparations, but because of the pressure exerted by various of the wartime allies against Japan, there were provisions for reparations in the final treaty. The cleverest of Dulles' innovations, from a legal point of view, was his suggestion of procedure regarding Chinese representation, but this was made obsolete by the entrance of the Chinese Communists into the Korean War.

THE MISSION OF JOHN FOSTER DULLES

Dulles' Visit to Japan and the Outbreak of the Korean War

The great advantages of Dulles' position over that of the planners of the State Department in the preparation of the Japanese peace treaty lay not so much in his conception of the treaty, which was not very different from theirs, but in the fact that he was one man—not a committee or a staff—who maintained all the necessary lines of communication with everyone who had a voice in the treaty; and in the further fact that at crucial points he was empowered by the President to mediate between conflicting points of view. In order to establish the requisite lines of communication, Dulles traveled very widely during his mission, beginning with a trip to Japan between the 14th and the 29th of June 1950.

In Tokyo Dulles discussed the treaty with General MacArthur. Apparently the temperaments and ideologies of the two men were well matched; at any rate, in their later relationship they expressed the highest esteem for each other. MacArthur, as we have seen, had advocated peace with Japan as early as 1947, and, in contrast to the military departments, he had consistently favored an almost complete restoration of sovereignty to the Japanese. His ideas on the timing of the treaty also essentially agreed with those of Dulles, for MacArthur felt that the Japanese deserved a settlement after six years of excellent behavior, and that if it were delayed their gratitude would gradually turn to rancor.

A fortunate circumstance for Dulles' program was the coincidence of his visit to Japan with a mission headed by Secretary of Defense Louis Johnson and Chairman of the Joint Chiefs of Staff Omar Bradley, the purpose of which was to study the military aspects of a peace settlement with Japan. This enabled Dulles and MacArthur to exchange views with the highest officials of the Pentagon, and possibly to reconcile them somewhat to an early treaty. (James Reston reported that these conversations resulted in agreement that work on the peace treaty should proceed even after the beginning of the Korean War,[6] but subsequent behavior of the Defense Department indicates that the agreement probably was incomplete.)

Dulles also held conversations with a number of prominent Japanese, both inside and outside the regime. He found many of the Japanese vague on methods of guarding Japan's security. Yoshida himself had no concrete program and would not commit himself on bases, though Dulles had the impression that Yoshida would acquiesce on this point. Many leaders clung, rather desperately, to the idea that the constitutional renunciation of war would provide safety. Only one of the labor leaders with whom Dulles spoke wished to see Japan rearmed, and he also found one of the more radical labor leaders expressing the opinion that the United States was in favor of rearming Japan only in the interest of American security. The divergence and vagueness of Japanese opinion worried Dulles, for he felt that negotiation and ratification of a treaty and a security agreement by the Japanese government would, in the long run, prove to be insufficient unless most of the country strongly concurred. He lectured Japanese political leaders on the need to establish a unified approach to foreign policy.

On June 25, 1950, in the middle of Dulles' visit to Japan, the armies of the Communist government of North Korea invaded South Korea. Five days later, Dulles was back in the United States. The personal relations established during his visit had added strength to his conviction that Japan must be given full and early opportunity to become an equal partner in the community of free nations. In the attack on South Korea, he saw a Soviet attempt to check the steps being taken by the United States toward this end, and he urged that peace-making with Japan should not be delayed by the war thus provoked.[7]

[6] *New York Times*, July 10, 1950, 1:3.
[7] DSB, xxiii, No. 575 (July 10, 1950), pp. 49-50.

THE MISSION OF JOHN FOSTER DULLES

There were many in the Pentagon who saw in the move of the Communists the intent to increase the encirclement of Japan and thus to keep her out of the camp of the Western powers. Some of these argued that no further step should be taken toward drafting a Japanese peace treaty until after the Korean War was over, on the ground that our military position in Japan under the Occupation was far superior to what it would be under any conceivable peace settlement. Dulles, however, continued to urge that the Korean crisis was even more reason for hastening the conclusion of the peace treaty, since the Japanese were awakening to the threat of Communist expansionism and would be more anxious than ever to regain their sovereignty under the terms offered by the Western powers.

On his return to the United States Dulles stepped up his timetable for the negotiation of the treaty. Within a month (August 7, 1950) he and his associates had completed a shortened draft of the document and had circulated it among various officials of the Department of State and the Pentagon. Three more drafts were produced in August and September by Dulles and his staff. The draft of August 7 was similar to prior drafts except that various detailed provisions had been omitted. The other three embodied some suggestions from Dulles' associates, including reinstatement of some provisions omitted in the draft of August 7.

At this time the successive drafts included in the section on security a provision for keeping American military forces on Japanese soil. The drafting of this provision had presented some difficult problems. In the first place, Article 1 had recognized the full sovereignty of the Japanese people over Japan and its territorial waters. To provide in the same treaty that the military power of Japan would be primarily in the hands of the United States seemed inconsistent to many people, since the country which controlled the military power in Japan would presumably be in a position to dictate the conditions under which sovereignty could be exercised.

Theoretically it is possible for a nation, while retaining formal sovereignty, to ask another nation or nations for military protection against other powers. Neutralized states have often done this in the past. In the case of a single powerless state asking protection from a powerful one, the degree of sovereignty left to the former would seem to depend upon the motivation for forbearance on the part of the latter in intervening in the exercise of sovereignty.

In the case of Japan seeking protection from the United States, there was good reason to rely on the forbearance of the United States in encroaching on the sovereignty of Japan. A main purpose of the peace settlement was to demonstrate to Japan and others that the United States was prepared and even eager to deal with her on the basis of full sovereignty and independence, in order to win the good will of the Japanese and keep them on the side of the free nations. The strength of this motivation was such that Japan would appear to be running little risk to her sovereignty in letting the United States provide her with military protection.

In place of requiring Japan, as a condition of peace, to allow American troops to remain indefinitely in Japanese territory, the proposed treaty provision was put in the form of a request by Japan for American military aid and an acceptance by the United States. This appeared to give Japan the initiative in the arrangement and hence did not formally impair the grant of full sovereignty to Japan.

A second question that could have been raised about the provision of American military aid, but that actually received very little attention at the time, was the effect of atomic warfare on the defense of offshore islands. In the course of 1950 it became known that Soviet Russia had broken the American monopoly of the atom bomb and was in fact beginning to manufacture its own bombs. The Japanese Islands were of

THE MISSION OF JOHN FOSTER DULLES

course within easy bombing range of Soviet Russia. Did this not mean that Japan would immediately be a prime target in any war between the United States and the Sino-Soviet bloc? In view of the distances involved, would it be possible in any case for the United States to protect Japan against intolerable war damage? Yet little was said at the time about these problems in the public discussions of the security provisions of the treaty. The main concern of the Japanese people seemed to be to avoid the granting of fixed military and naval bases on Japanese soil for an indefinite period of time. This fear was met in part by providing that, for the purpose of maintaining international peace, American troops would be used anywhere in Japan where they might be needed. It was emphasized that this arrangement was comparable to that which enabled United States forces to be stationed in Britain.

In a press conference on September 14, 1950, President Truman announced that the State Department was authorized to initiate further discussions with the member nations of the Far Eastern Commission in regard to a peace treaty with Japan. He recalled that the United States had first made an effort in 1947 to call such a conference, but that procedural difficulties had prevented any progress. He stated that this decision was "in accord with the general effort of the United States to bring to an end all war situations," such as securing a peace pact for Austria and concluding the state of war with Germany.[8] This announcement was followed by the circulation of a seven-point memorandum to the FEC members on the suggested content of the treaty.[9]

The first of the seven points laid down the principle that the parties to the treaty should be "any or all nations at war with Japan which are willing to make peace on the basis proposed

[8] *New York Times*, September 15, 1950, 1:5, reporting Truman's statement of September 14, 1950.
[9] This document was made public on November 24, 1950, only after the Soviet Union had published its reply. The intention had been to keep the discussions confidential.

107

and as may be agreed." It left little doubt that the United States was by that time quite prepared to make peace without the Soviet Union if the latter should prove obdurate in its resistance to American and Allied ideas as to procedure or substance. Five of the remaining six points have already been mentioned as forming part of Dulles' first conception of the treaty. These were Japanese membership in the United Nations; retention of United States "and perhaps other forces" in Japan, pending effective security arrangements within the United Nations organization; adherence by Japan to treaties touching narcotics, fisheries, and international trade; mutual waiver of claims; and reference of disputes to the International Court of Justice. The other point, numbered third in the list, had to do with territory, and had been modified to satisfy the Department of Defense. In the earliest version, Japan was required to "accept any decision of the United Nations which extends the trustee system to all or part of the Ryukyu and Bonin Islands." The modified formula required Japan to "agree to United Nations trusteeship, with the United States as administering authority, of the Ryukyu and Bonin Islands." The clauses calling for Japanese recognition of the independence of Korea and acceptance of "the future decision of the United Kingdom, the U.S.S.R., China, and the U.S. with reference to the status of Formosa, the Pescadores, South Sakhalin, and the Kuriles" were unchanged from the first draft. Japan's renunciation of special rights and interests in China was new.

At a press conference on the day following the President's announcement, Dulles made public the fact that the United States was not proposing any restriction on rearmament in Japan. He also revealed the possibility that a new kind of procedure might be employed in negotiating the treaty. Owing to the special circumstances of the case, there might be no peace conference. The business might be done by a series of bilateral discussions with the governments concerned.[10]

[10] It was even thought at one time that these discussions would

THE MISSION OF JOHN FOSTER DULLES

Dulles did not on this occasion give specific reasons for avoiding a general conference. The impossibility of agreement with the Soviet Union as to who should participate and how decisions should be reached might have been justification enough. Furthermore, if a peace conference were convened, which government would represent China? There was a split in the FEC countries between those who continued to recognize the Nationalist government and those who had recognized the Communist regime. The suggestion of bilateral discussion made it fairly clear that the treaty would be concluded only with such countries as could agree with the United States on the terms.

The General Assembly of the United Nations was in session in New York throughout the autumn of 1950. Taking advantage of this fact, Dulles and John Allison, Director of the Office of Northeast Asian Affairs in the State Department, held conversations with representatives of all the countries represented in the FEC on the basis of the Seven-Point Memorandum. Indonesia was brought into consultation in the same way, and before the end of the year Ceylon was added to the list.

The representatives of Australia, New Zealand, and the Philippines objected to the absence of restrictions on Japanese rearmament and to the waiver of reparations. Burma joined in the protest on the first point and Nationalist China on the second. On the first point, however, there was already talk of compensation in the form of security treaties which would bind the United States to give assistance in the event of attack by a remilitarized Japan, and this was the solution eventually adopted. As we shall see, the reparations issue proved less amenable to compromise. Although Australia and New Zealand were later brought around to the American point of view, the Philippines refused to go along, and this point resulted in

result in a number of identical bilateral treaties rather than one general treaty.

a delay in ratification of the treaty by the Philippines. Unsatisfied reparations claims were also among the reasons invoked for Indonesia's delay. The United Kingdom expressed a desire to curtail Japan's dominance in Far Eastern trade. The representatives of Canada, India, and Pakistan undertook, with little or no comment, to transmit the views of the United States to their respective governments. The Dutch and French representatives expressed general agreement with the American proposals.

General opposition to the proposed draft came only from the delegation of the Soviet Union. This was of course not unexpected, since Malik had put the Soviet position clearly in his conversation with Dulles on October 26, 1950.

Dulles indicated that he understood this situation from the beginning. His plans were made without any illusion that the USSR could be induced to be a party to them. There was no use in trying to offer any special concessions to buy Soviet participation, since the basic issue of Japan's role as a member of the Western alliance offered no opportunity for compromise. Dulles accordingly confined his efforts to making the proper formal move toward inviting Russian participation, while remaining alert to the possibility that the Russian leaders would resort to wrecking tactics.

The Kremlin promptly sought to take advantage of Dulles' proffered seven-point plan to confuse the whole issue of the settlement. In an aide-mémoire of November 20, 1950, the Kremlin posed certain questions, as indicated in the following numbered paragraphs:[11]

(1) The signatories of the Declaration by United Nations made in Washington on New Year's Day, 1942, undertook not to conclude peace separately. Did the United States possibly contemplate a treaty in which only some of those signatories would participate?

[11] Unofficial translation in DSB, XXIII, No. 596 (December 4, 1950), pp. 881-82.

(2) The Cairo Declaration of December 1, 1943, and the Potsdam Declaration of July 26, 1945, decided the question of the restoration of Formosa and the Pescadores to China. The Yalta Agreement of February 11, 1945, returned the southern part of Sakhalin, and gave the Kuriles to the Soviet Union. What then was the meaning of the clause in the memorandum which would make the status of all these territories subject to a new decision?

(3) Neither at Cairo nor at Potsdam had there been any question of removing the Ryukyu and Bonin Islands from Japanese sovereignty. The governments participating in both of these acts had announced that they "had no thoughts of territorial expansion."[12] What then was the basis for the proposal to place these islands under trusteeship, with the United States administering them for the United Nations?

(4) The Japanese people were deeply interested in the withdrawal of the Occupation forces, as provided in paragraph 12 of the Potsdam Declaration. Would the treaty lay down a definite period for withdrawal, as those concluded with former enemy states in Europe had done?

(5) The FEC's Basic Post-Surrender Policy of June 19, 1947, prohibited any army, navy, or air force for Japan. Under the heading of security, Point 4 of the American memorandum mentioned joint responsibility between Japanese facilities[13] and United States and perhaps other forces. Did this mean (a) that Japanese forces were to be created, and (b) that after the peace American military, naval, and air force bases would be maintained in Japanese territory?

(6) The memorandum had nothing to say on securing for Japan the opportunity to develop her peacetime economy. Was

[12] This occurs in the Statement of December 1, 1943, on the Cairo Conference.

[13] By translating this with the Russian word for "organs," the Soviet government strengthened the implication that the United States was planning to stimulate the development of Japanese military, naval, and air forces and staff. There were of course some grounds for such an extensive interpretation.

it intended to include, in the treaty, clauses removing all limitations on such development, as well as granting access to raw materials and participation with equal rights in world trade?

(7) China had suffered years of aggression at the hands of Japanese militarists and had therefore a special interest in the settlement with Japan. What was being done to ascertain the views of the government of the Chinese People's Republic?

This was a characteristic effort on the part of the Kremlin to confuse the issue. Without any embarrassing commitment, and merely by queries, it assumed the appealing posture of champion of Japanese aspirations to independence and welfare. At the same time, while insinuating that the trusteeship of the Bonin and Ryukyu Islands would be merely a disguise for the usurpation of sovereignty by the United States and thus a violation of the principle of non-territorial expansion, it carefully safeguarded its own expansion in Sakhalin and the Kuriles. The quiet assumption that the righteousness of its own acquisitions was beyond question, while any made by its erstwhile allies would be highly reprehensible, was of course not peculiar to Soviet diplomacy. What was perhaps new was the nakedness of this effort to make the best of two worlds.

Shortly afterward the United States published its answer to the queries of the Soviet government.[14] This was designed, not to convince the Soviets, which was impossible, but to reduce the propaganda value of the Russian position. The answer pointed out that the undertaking not to make separate peace had been designed to keep the coalition together until victory had been won. This purpose had long ago been achieved, and the United States could not accept an interpretation of the obligation which would make it possible for any single power to hold up indefinitely a peace settlement. As for the territorial agreements made at Yalta, the United States government had always held that these were subject to confirmation

[14] Department of State Press Release, No. 1267, December 28, 1950.

in a peace treaty to be concluded in consultation with states that had taken part in the war against Japan. It would, further, be well within the powers of the victors to put the Bonin and Ryukyu Islands under trusteeship, since the Potsdam Proclamation had specifically laid it down that, of the minor islands held by Japan, only those determined by the United States, Great Britain, and China should be restored to Japanese sovereignty. The United States did not understand the Soviet suggestion that this would amount to territorial expansion on the part of the state chosen to administer the United Nations trust. The views of the Chinese People's Republic were not being consulted because the United States, like a majority of the other states that had fought against Japan, did not recognize the Communists as the government of China. As for the other Soviet queries, touching upon the creation of Japanese forces and the retention of American bases in Japanese territory, the United States felt that the memorandum itself provided sufficient answer.

The Soviet queries on the Seven-Point Memorandum were designed merely to muddy the waters and reflected no intention on the part of the Kremlin to advance the drafting of a Japanese peace treaty. The case was different with the replies received from the other nations that had participated in the war against Japan.

Of these, India took the most critical stand in regard to the American memorandum. Some of its criticism, moreover, was identical with that from Moscow. The Indian government, like the Soviets, was unwilling to see the Yalta decisions on Sakhalin and the Kuriles reopened. To this the reply was made that the United States would advocate confirmation of Soviet title in a peace treaty participated in by the Soviet Union, but saw no point in rendering this service to Moscow if it remained aloof. The Indian government also thought that the Bonin and Ryukyu Islands should be left under the unqualified sovereignty of Japan, and that Formosa and the Pescadores should be restored to the Chinese People's Republic. It was against any provision in the treaty itself for the retention of Allied troops on Japanese territory, since, in its view, this meant taking advantage of a temporary weakness that would be lastingly resented. On the other hand, it was prepared, after the treaty came into force, to see Japan enter into security arrangements with the United States or other powers. It was willing to waive reparations, but it held that Japan should be prevented from rearming, although it did not wish to impose a control that would interfere in domestic affairs. It wanted the treaty to be drawn up in a conference of all the FEC states, with the Communist government representing China; but it differed from the Soviet Union as to voting, being willing to accept the American proposal that matters of substance be decided by a two-thirds majority. Thus, while the Indian government advocated various concessions to the Russians, its position in regard to the voting on the treaty terms would have given the deciding power to the Western states and would have been completely unacceptable to Moscow.

The attitude of the Chinese Nationalist government at this stage merits some comment. It did not withdraw its proposal of 1947 that the four Great Powers should each have a veto in the proceedings of the proposed peace conference. But its dependence on the United States for the maintenance of its position in Formosa and for any hope of recovering its status on the mainland made it loath to oppose American ideas on the substance of the settlement. By December 1950, it was willing to waive reparations if the other nations did. It concurred in the proposed security arrangements, including United States trusteeship in the Bonin and Ryukyu Islands. Most notable of all, it was prepared to see the future of Formosa left undecided, provided Japan renounced all title thereto. On these points it was being a good ally of the United States, but the problem still remained of how the other states could be induced to consent to its representing China for the purposes of the treaty.

THE MISSION OF JOHN FOSTER DULLES

The views of the British Commonwealth governments regarding the nature of the Japanese peace settlement were of special interest to Dulles and his colleagues. They had already been in possession of detailed information regarding these views some months before the conversations took place on the Seven-Point Memorandum. A Working Party set up in pursuance of a decision taken at the Colombo Conference had met in London from May 1 to May 17, 1950, some four months before the circulation of the Seven-Point Memorandum, and the United States had received a reasonably full account of its deliberations.

The delegations from Australia, Canada, Ceylon, India, New Zealand, Pakistan, South Africa, and the United Kingdom, making up the Working Party, had manifested much good will, mingled with anxiety over what they believed to be the trends in American thought touching the terms of settlement with Japan. All were conscious of the great preponderance of the United States' share in the responsibility for peace in the Pacific, all knew how the American taxpayer had footed and was still footing the bill for the occupation and the rehabilitation of Japan, all were sensible of their countries' actual and potential debt to the United States, most were too wise to take stands which they had reason to believe would be sharply antipathetic to official American opinion. However, they desired to get plainly on the record their several ideas as to what the major terms of settlement should be, hoping that due consideration would be given to them. In this they were not doomed to complete disappointment. Of all the members of the Commonwealth who eventually signed the peace treaty at San Francisco, those who were left with the greatest misgivings were Australia and New Zealand. But they at least had the satisfaction, before going to San Francisco, of personal discussion with the American negotiators, from whom they received full and sympathetic explanations of the positions taken by the United States.

THE MISSION OF JOHN FOSTER DULLES

All of the members of the Working Party were of one mind that no country then represented on the FEC should be left out in the drafting of a treaty. Ceylon and perhaps Indochina should be added. Both the Soviet Union and the Chinese People's Republic should take part unless it was made quite clear that they would not do so on terms acceptable to the democratic powers. How to bring the Chinese People's Republic in was a question for which no confident answer could be found. Obviously the convening power ought to be the United States, which, like Canada, Australia, New Zealand, France, and the Philippines, had not recognized Mao Tse-tung and his current colleagues as constituting the government of China.

The problem that attracted most attention was again, as at Canberra, post-treaty security. This time, however, there was nothing like the same concentration on the danger of renewed Japanese aggression. In the intervening two and a half years, even the Pacific Dominions had gained some appreciation of the importance of keeping Japan's manpower and productive capacity off the Russian side in the balance of power. Three alternative ways of doing this were considered.

One way would be a general pact guaranteeing and organizing the defense of Japan. But the likelihood that Soviet Russia and Communist China would join in such a pact on terms acceptable to the democracies was felt to be slight. If they did, they would undoubtedly take advantage of their geographic proximity to dominate Japan.

Another possibility was an agreement among all the peacemaking powers besides the Soviet Union and Communist China. In the eyes of the members of the Working Party, the value of this would depend upon the certainty of concrete and defined contributions from all parties. Yet it was feared that an attack on Japan might come as one phase of a general war to which the resources of the Pacific Dominions would already be fully committed. Moreover, there might be strong popular feeling in Australia and New Zealand against any responsibility for the security of a former enemy, especially if the two Dominions were themselves not explicitly guaranteed against attack.

The third solution considered (and this was thought the most practical) was a bilateral defense pact between the United States and Japan. However, there was a risk attached to this proposal. In order to lighten its unilateral responsibility, the United States might build up Japanese land, sea, and air forces and armaments to the point where aggression would again be an imminent possibility. With military assistance in view, the United States would conceivably oppose any restriction in the treaty on Japanese rearmament. Some of the Commonwealth countries were opposed to raising Japanese defense forces even under a bilateral security pact.

Actually the Working Party did not place itself without hedging behind any of these alternatives. It was, after all, taking great care not to foreclose independent judgment by each of the Commonwealth governments. Worth noting, however, was the statement made on behalf of Australia that any kind of security arrangement that would keep the United States forces in Japan would go far to allay her fears of a rebirth of Japanese militarism. From the beginning to the end of negotiations, Australia, supported by New Zealand, was to prove most insistent on safeguards against what she considered a very real danger.

There was some discussion of preventing Japanese rearmament, not by means of irritating internal controls, but by the long-range allocation of raw materials. One defect in such a device would be that China and the Soviet Union would probably furnish many of the materials which the democratic countries most wanted to cut off. The Australian, New Zealand, and South African delegations appeared to share the view that any screening of imports would have to be supplemented by a more or less energetic control mechanism established in Japan. The United Kingdom and Canada were represented as increasingly skeptical regarding the efficacy of physical controls in Japan, while India, Ceylon, and Pakistan finally joined in the vague opinion that the solution of the security problem was to be found in some form of multilateral organization that would not interfere in Japanese domestic affairs. These countries showed no reluctance to make demands regarding treaty terms that could not by any stretch of the imagination be accepted by the interested powers, or that ignored the realities of the international political world. The making of demands for ideal solutions is a luxury which, in general, only those nations which have no responsibility for carrying out the demands can afford.

In the matter of economic restrictions, there were some signs of at least a change in emphasis since the Canberra meeting. It is true that if all the restrictions proposed by individual delegations were added up, they would have constituted a formidable barrier to any kind of Japanese economic recovery. But there was no easy acceptance of these proposals, and there was a fuller appreciation of the difficulty of imposing restrictions without so depressing the Japanese economy as to make the country an easy prey to communism. When the suggestion was made that the best way to prevent Japan from returning to the unfair trading practices and cut-throat competition of the prewar period might be a voluntary undertaking on her part to continue observing certain of the Occupation codes, the idea was not laughed out of court. It would probably have had short shrift at Canberra in 1947.

When the Working Party took up the territorial provisions of a future treaty, they were again confronted by the specter of two Chinas. The Commonwealth countries were themselves divided on the recognition of the Chinese People's Republic, and they had to reckon with the possibility that the United States would continue to stand out for Chiang Kai-shek. The majority, moreover, irrespective of recognition, were loath to see more territory brought under Communist control. Most of the delegations were therefore content that the treaty should merely require Japanese renunciation of title to Formosa and the Pescadores, without specification of ultimate disposal. This would leave to time, or to post-treaty negotiation, the question as to which "republic" of China was to receive these islands.

In regard to the Bonin and Ryukyu Islands, it was generally believed, as it had been at Canberra, that the United States would retain control, possibly in the form of a strategic trusteeship, which could be justified in the United Nations as a guard against Japanese aggression. Strategic trusteeships, of course, fell under the jurisdiction of the Security Council, where the Soviet veto might well prove an insuperable obstacle. The alternative of an ordinary trusteeship under the General Assembly was considered, but no decided preference was indicated.

One treaty clause which seems to have had its genesis in the Working Party's deliberations is the paragraph in Article 2 of the treaty where Japan renounced all claim to any interest in the Antarctic area. Australia, New Zealand, and South Africa joined in urging this exclusion, apparently on security grounds. Security again, as well as the conservation of resources, was cited as a reason for bringing Japanese whaling and fishing under international regulation. The suggestion was made that a conference might be convened to allocate fishing areas in the Far East.

Reparations were described as "largely a dead issue." It was agreed that nothing further should be taken from industrial equipment in Japan, and that reparations from current production would be incompatible with a tolerable standard of living in Japan. This left only gold and external assets. Both should be available for reparations, even Japanese holdings in neutral countries. There was apparently a strong feeling against allowing either gold or external assets to be earmarked for Occupation costs.

Survivals from the Canberra Conference were the proposals that the treaty should require Japan to prevent undesirable political associations, and to maintain and enforce a code of human rights. The primary purpose of the last-named proposal was to secure proper treatment of aliens in Japan. The precedent in mind was the group of European "satellite" treaties; but their actual enforcement was hoped for in this case. The only suggestion of how such a hope might be realized was to make it clear in the treaty that if Japan failed to name an arbiter to settle a dispute arising out of the Human Rights clauses, the Secretary-General of the United Nations should have power to name one for her. Thus the textual weakness in the "satellite" treaties, which had been referred to the International Court of Justice for an advisory opinion, and which was to lead the Court to deny the Secretary-General's authority to appoint even a third arbiter unless both parties had made their appointments,[15] would have been avoided. This improvement, however, would hardly have solved the problem of actual enforcement.

When, as the fall of 1950 wore on, Great Britain was pressed for her views on the Seven-Point Memorandum, the Foreign Office complained of a lack of detail in the document, and suggested that the much fuller report of the Commonwealth Working Party should serve as the basis of further discussion. The report, it pointed out, had been given the State Department in September, but no comment had been received.

The American officials objected to using the report as a basis of discussion, on the ground that half a year had passed since the meeting of the Commonwealth delegations, and that in the interval opinions would, it was to be hoped, have moved ahead. They indicated that the American Seven-Point Memorandum covered succinctly all the matters which, in the con-

[15] *Interpretation of Peace Treaties with Bulgaria, Hungary and Rumania*, International Court of Justice Reports, 1950, pp. 221-61. The opinion was handed down on July 18, 1950.

sidered judgment of the United States government, should be dealt with in the treaty. The differences between the Memorandum and the Working Party's report consisted in the omission from the former of many points discussed in the latter. The omissions were intentional and meant that, in the view now held by the United States, these points should not enter into the treaty. It was more than hinted that to resume discussions at the stage represented by the Working Party's report would be a step backward—a retreat toward restrictions and controls which the American negotiators considered out of keeping with the progress made by Japan under the Occupation and with developments in the contemporary world conflict.

The Working Party's report probably had some quite undesigned effects. It revealed not only a continuing confusion of aims, but considerable difference within the Commonwealth, together with some lack of confidence in the validity of the positions taken. No one could read the document at all carefully without surmising that a stiff and united front would be presented on very few of the points of difference with the United States. The American negotiators may well have been strengthened in the belief that the simple and liberal treaty which they now thought so desirable was a practical possibility. If so, further reinforcement was shortly forthcoming in the form of unofficial conversations with officials of the Foreign Office in London and in Tokyo. These clearly indicated that the United Kingdom at least would not oppose Japanese rearmament, and would probably not press very hard even for economic restrictions. It was, moreover, prepared to use its influence with the other members of the Commonwealth in the direction of a short and liberal treaty, which would do little more than end the state of war and prepare the way for Japan's entry into the United Nations and other international organizations. The Commonwealth Prime Ministers were meeting in London in January 1951, and this would provide an opportunity for sounding out opinion.

Against the background of all this information, the conviction, rooted in the minds of some high officers of the Occupation, that the British would do their utmost to prevent the United States from getting the kind of peace it wanted must have seemed a trifle gratuitous. Pretty clearly, this idea was a reflection of local tensions, not a conclusion reached after a detached and comprehensive survey of the forces operating upon the several governments of the Commonwealth. British representatives in Tokyo from time to time irritated SCAP with questions that implied some criticism of particular measures and some skepticism about the results claimed for the Occupation in general. In turn, they were irritated (not without grounds acknowledged by some American observers) by an attitude which seemed to imply that any critical inquiry amounted to something like *lèse-majesté* tinged with blasphemy. Had this tension communicated itself to the principal British and American negotiators, there might well have been no treaty.

CHAPTER VI

DIRECT NEGOTIATIONS ON THE TREATY

FOLLOWING the conversations with the delegates to the General Assembly of the United Nations, Dulles embarked on a voyage of direct negotiation with the Allied governments on the specific details of the proposed treaty. To the Philippine government, which he next visited, the most important features of the prospective peace settlement were, first, reparations and, second, security. Against the equity of the Philippine demands on these subjects, Dulles had no argument. The Japanese had been driven out of the Philippines in 1944, but their devastations were still everywhere visible; while the cruelties, humiliations, and casualties of their occupation of the country would be a bitter memory for many years to come. The apostle of a magnanimous peace had to rely for justification upon economic reason and the imperious political needs of the free world.

In regard to reparations, Dulles brought up the familiar argument that a large reparations bill forced on Japan would only bring unemployment and starvation to that country and in the end would be defaulted. The only alternative was that the bill might be paid by the United States, which was out of the question. He was given a courteous hearing, but he realized that he had not persuaded either the Philippine government or the legislature to waive the claim for eight billion dollars of compensation. The mood of the Philippines, he reported in a radio address of March 1, 1951,[1] was like that of France in 1919. Arguments about the need to permit Japan to have a viable economy so that she could act as a bulwark against the advance of Russian imperialism made little headway against

[1] DSB, xxiv, No. 610 (March 12, 1951), p. 405.

DIRECT NEGOTIATIONS ON THE TREATY

the daily reminders of the aching ruins of Manila as compared with what seemed to be a rapid recovery in Tokyo. As is often the case everywhere, the pressing problems of the day tended to obscure long-range contingencies.

In the matter of security, the Ambassador was hardly more successful in persuasion. The Filipinos were primarily concerned with protection from a possible renewal of Japanese aggression. In Japan, Dulles had offered a bilateral security pact; but, while this could be and was justified as a remedy for the post-treaty defenselessness of a disarmed country, it was also designed to meet the strategic requirements of the United States in defending the offshore island chain. In the Philippines, strategic needs were already met by the arrangements for bases for the United States which had survived the transfer of sovereignty.

When he undertook his mission, Dulles had been instructed to negotiate a regional security pact for the Pacific. This would naturally have included the Philippines, but Dulles had learned that the British were not going to welcome any pact which covered the Philippines without also taking in Malaya and Hong Kong. If these were included, the French and Dutch would probably expect similar protection for their interests in the area, and such a commitment was far broader than the United States military authorities wanted to make. When, therefore, the Philippine government raised the question of post-treaty controls to prevent the resurgence of aggressive forces in Japan, Dulles was not in a position to offer any specific alternative guarantee. All that he could do for the moment was to insist that the crux of the security problem was how to prevent the Soviet Union from adding the great potentialities of Japan to her own and those of Communist China for an expansionist drive that would stop at no limits in Asia or the South Pacific. A treaty that would make a friend of Japan would go farther to keep her on our side than a host of galling and unenforceable controls.

DIRECT NEGOTIATIONS ON THE TREATY

From Manila Mr. Dulles went on to Canberra, where he spent four days in conference with Prime Minister Menzies, Mr. Spender, Minister of External Affairs, some other members of the Australian cabinet, and Mr. Doidge, New Zealand's Minister of External Affairs. Reports concerning the meeting of Commonwealth Prime Ministers in London early in January had led him to expect stubborn opposition in this quarter, especially on the question of post-treaty controls in Japan. Australians and New Zealanders were still, in February 1951, more afraid of Japan than of Russia. They were still demanding effective measures on the spot to prevent the reestablishment of aggressively nationalistic societies in Japan, the accumulation of Japanese armaments, and the restoration of the old militaristic cliques. They also wanted at least enough reparations to provide pecuniary compensation to prisoners of war who had suffered from the savage barbarity of Japanese prison compounds.

Again Dulles found the mood like that of France in 1919. He was caricatured in Australian newspapers as a combination of Yankee missionary, deluded by Japanese pretenses of reform and eager to help "the little brother," and American imperialist, determined to use Japan for the political and economic expansion of the United States. Yet when he left Canberra and Wellington, he was far more confident than he had been on leaving Manila that his talks had done something to change outlooks and soften resistance. Indeed, the other participants themselves acknowledged the influence of his courteous but forceful arguments. His visit served in large measure to change their problem to that of persuading their electorates. For this task he had, moreover, provided effective assistance by opening up the prospect of a security pact.

During this trip of Dulles', the problem of security in the Far East began to overshadow all other aspects of the peace settlement. The tension between the free states and the Soviet group had mounted to a high pitch, and a general war had at

DIRECT NEGOTIATIONS ON THE TREATY

times seemed very close. The American policy-makers who tried to get a global perspective on this menacing situation were generally impressed by the need to restore some semblance of a balance of power in the Far East as a deterrent to further efforts at expansion by the Communist nations.

The first thing to be noticed in any such enterprise was the lack of exportable military power in the non-Communist countries of the area. In spite of large populations and extensive territories, they had surprisingly little to throw in as a counterweight to Communist power, even if they had wanted to do so. They were all suffering from mass poverty, shortage of resources, and lack of skills. Those states which had recently emerged from dependence to a status of freedom seemed only to have increased their internal instability.

This situation would normally have rendered hopeless the effort to create a working equilibrium. But the astonishing improvement in the technology of warfare had made it possible for Great Powers to exercise their military strength at long distances from the home territory. The United States had given an undeniably impressive exhibition of overwhelming power exerted five thousand miles from home. The new dimensions which military potential had acquired meant that systems of equilibrium were no longer tied to particular geographical regions. The full force of United States military power could be thrown into the scales halfway around the globe. However, there was a grave question as to whether this alone, because of the immensely difficult problems of logistics involved, would be sufficient to counterbalance Communist power in the Far East, and also whether the people of the United States were prepared to exert their full power to protect people of other cultures in such distant lands. Erecting a balance of power in the Far East could obviously not be reduced to a simple equation of Soviet-Chinese power on the one hand and American power on the other.

DIRECT NEGOTIATIONS ON THE TREATY

Under the circumstances, what could Dulles do? At least two alternatives presented themselves. One was to build up Japanese strength and to do everything possible to keep Japan on our side. The second was to try to detach Communist China from the Soviet orbit and return it to its former position on the Anglo-American side of the balance.

To many people this second alternative had great attraction. Communist China was many times the size of Japan in territory and manpower, and vastly richer in natural resources. Although she had been weak in the past, she was rapidly finding herself as a nation and developing a certain cohesion. If she could be taken out of the Communist orbit and counted on the other side, the whole balance-of-power picture would be radically changed.

The fact that the Communist regime was apparently firmly established in China was not then regarded as an insuperable obstacle to effecting such a change. The case of Tito's Yugoslavia seemed to show that it was possible to separate a former satellite state with a Communist government from bondage to the Kremlin, and even to line it up with the free states in opposition to Russian expansion. It was likewise argued that there were many points at which the interests of Peiping and Moscow were really in conflict, and under the proper conditions these might cause a definite break between the two countries. If this could be brought about, the fact that within her borders the Chinese still maintained a Communist system should not be permitted to stand in the way of this solution to the power problem. On the other hand, if we assumed a permanent non-recognition policy toward the Peiping regime, we would thereby consolidate a Russian-Chinese coalition regardless of the two great nations' conflicts of interest, and this coalition would outweigh all alternative possibilities of power-balancing in Asia.

But whatever might have been the calculation of the pros and cons of working China into the balance of power in 1949,

DIRECT NEGOTIATIONS ON THE TREATY

by the time Dulles took up consideration of the security problem such calculations were politically impossible. Furthermore, the entrance of Chinese forces directly into the Korean hostilities in December 1950 gave a strong moral basis to the case against rewarding aggression with recognition. Once the consolidation of Peiping and Moscow had become firmly fixed, there was considerable risk in trying to get China over to our side by offering concessions which strengthened her. If she took the concessions and still did not come over, it would be too late for us to retract them.

The other Pacific nations which had suffered from Japanese attacks during the war were far removed from Russia and much less concerned about the necessity for building up effective strength against her. They were inclined to believe that the United States would protect them against the Soviet Union in any case. Their real fear was that a revived and rearmed Japan would again be looking for room to expand in the South Pacific. They therefore held out strongly for rigorous controls over Japanese rearmament. To Dulles' argument that this would only drive Japan into the camp of the Soviet Union and China, they answered that if no controls were instituted, Japan could pretend to be on the Western side and then, after rearming, could swing over to the Communist camp.

Actually the statesmen of Australia and New Zealand knew that, since the United States was contributing most of the power and the leadership, the security problem would have to be looked at from her point of view. If they refused to do this and insisted on their own conception of the security problem, they would end up by facing a combination of Russia, China, and Japan. They were accordingly prepared to go along with the kind of a peace treaty the United States wanted, without the maintenance of controls over Japan, but for their own protection they desired a security pact that would bring the United States to their aid against a revived and rearmed Japan.

DIRECT NEGOTIATIONS ON THE TREATY

Dulles' instructions from President Truman had contemplated the making of a Pacific security arrangement, but this was to be broader and more comprehensive than merely a three-party treaty, as desired by Australia and New Zealand. But both of these countries were extremely reluctant to enter into a security pact that included Japan as a party. In order to get the full support of both countries for his treaty of peace, Dulles agreed to submit a three-power security draft to the government at Washington for consideration.

On his return to the United States, Dulles broadcast a detailed report on the work of his mission to Japan.[2] He described the basic elements of the peace which the United States sought in the following terms:

(1) "The peace should restore Japan as an equal in the society of nations." This meant that Japan should not be subjected to restrictions of any kind on her sovereignty which other sovereign nations did not accept for themselves.

(2) "The peace should give Japan a chance to earn her way in the world and become self-sustaining." This did not call for an indefinite continuation of the United States subsidy. It did require that no heavy economic or financial burdens or major commercial disabilities would be placed upon Japan by the treaty and that Japan should have the opportunity to earn the means to buy abroad the food and raw materials necessary to enable her people to live and to work.

(3) "The peace should encourage close cultural relations between Japan and the West." This required special efforts to develop cultural and intellectual interchange between the two countries.

(4) "The peace should give Japan a reasonable degree of security." To this end the Japanese had been informed that, if they wanted it, the United States would sympathetically consider the retention of United States forces in Japan so that the

[2] Address made over the Columbia Broadcasting System on March 1, 1951. (*Ibid.*, pp. 403-7.)

DIRECT NEGOTIATIONS ON THE TREATY

coming into force of a treaty of peace would not leave Japan a vacuum of power into which Soviet communism would surely move. This was an invitation which Japan, according to Mr. Dulles, could accept or decline. At the same time, it was only on a provisional basis, and we could not permanently give any nation a "free ride" so far as its security was concerned.

After discussing in detail his conversations with the other countries in the Pacific area, he concluded that "We have now reached a point where it ought to be possible to draft promptly the actual text of a Japanese peace treaty which would genuinely promote peace in the Far East."

The Australian visit was hardly less profitable to the American peace mission than to the Australians and New Zealanders. It produced a swift clarification of ideas on the form, scope, and content of the security arrangements to be made in the Pacific. Except for the specification that the contemplated council was to consist of the foreign ministers or their deputies, and minor changes of wording regarding the functions of this council, the tripartite security treaty binding the United States, Australia, and New Zealand reached its final form at Canberra on February 17, 1951. The Pacific Dominions were by this time prepared to go ahead with an arrangement which would not include the United Kingdom, and, although London was slow and reluctant to signify the approval which the United States desired, this was the arrangement which prevailed. Mr. Spender, Australian Minister of External Affairs, was no less positive in this context than his Labour Party predecessor, Mr. Evatt, had been in others that in matters bearing directly on the interests of Australia and New Zealand, Downing Street must come around to the views firmly held by the governments of those Dominions.

Their views were even more opposed than those of the United States government to an indefinite extension of security obligations beyond the three nations. Canberra and Wellington

DIRECT NEGOTIATIONS ON THE TREATY

were very doubtful about the popular reception of any undertaking to come to the rescue of the late enemy, Japan. They were disinclined for the moment to bind themselves to defend the Philippines, Indonesia, or Indochina, though, but for opposition from the United Kingdom, they might have been persuaded to include the first-named. They were already committed to assist Great Britain in keeping the peace of the Middle East, and they were loath to assume duties which their already heavily taxed resources would not permit them to implement. The position which they took on these matters did much to exclude for the time being a general security pact for the Pacific and to fix instead the policy of separate agreements.

The tripartite treaty did not by any means offer everything that Australia and New Zealand desired. In case of threat to territorial integrity or political independence, the only clear obligation was to "consult together." Action was promised only in the event of armed attack, and even then was not necessarily military. Critics of the arrangement contrasted it unfavorably with the text of the North Atlantic Treaty, where "the use of armed force," although not strictly and legally obligatory, is at least explicitly mentioned. The formula used for the Anzus Pact was similar to that of the Rio Convention between the United States and its Latin American neighbors rather than to the North Atlantic Treaty. Dulles had been in the Senate at the time of the debates over the North Atlantic Treaty formula, and he knew that the Senate would be disinclined to ratify a similar formula for the Pacific area. Under the North Atlantic Treaty formula, armed force might be used without first obtaining Congressional assent in the particular case. Under the Monroe Doctrine type of agreement, that was not true. There was not the same necessity for it in the Pacific Pact, since there would normally be little difficulty in obtaining quick consent to the use of military force in the case of an attack upon Australia or New Zealand. In fact, it might be asked whether the pact guaranteed anything more than what the United States would be bound to do in its own interest irrespective of the treaty. But the public expression of this obligation went a long way in reconciling the people of Australia and New Zealand to a peace treaty which did not contain provisions for the continued and enforced disarmament of Japan.

In view of the deep impression that he made in Australia and New Zealand, it seems unfortunate that Dulles himself did not find it possible also to pay a visit to India. Independence was a new and prized possession for India, and its role in international politics had not yet been crystallized. Its internal problems were immensely complicated and the hope was that India could avoid becoming involved in the deepening struggle between the Communist and non-Communist world. It was widely believed that, unless India could get her own economic system in order within a few years, it would be impossible to escape revolution and chaos. This gave a strong impetus toward a neutral role for India and helped to engender a fear of being looked upon as a satellite of the United States. India, it was felt, must play the role of an Asiatic country and assist all other Asian countries to throw off Western leading-strings, as it itself had done. Aside from this, Prime Minister Nehru found some good things in the theory of communism, but not in Soviet totalitarianism. He knew that the interests of India would be better served by the Anglo-American bloc than by the Soviet Union and its allies, if a choice between them had to be made. It appeared that he had already gone part way toward making the choice, since India was accepting aid from Britain and the Dominions under the Colombo Plan, and from the United States under the Mutual Security Act and in a loan for the purchase of wheat. But, having done this, Nehru was disinclined to participate in a treaty for Japan that was obviously going to by-pass both the Soviet Union and Communist China. The reasons which he subsequently gave for the failure of India to go along with the settlement related to the

DIRECT NEGOTIATIONS ON THE TREATY

timing of the security arrangements and the content of some of the territorial clauses—questions largely of the prestige of Japan, on which he seemed to be more sensitive than most Japanese. The case he made might not at that time have been strong enough to resist the analytical and persuasive powers of Mr. Dulles in person. In any event, he might have gained a better understanding than he seems to have had of the real alternatives that Dulles was facing in negotiating a peace settlement.

The original conception of a Pacific security pact which Dulles had been authorized to discuss was one which brought together the obligations the United States already had or was prepared to take on in the Pacific area. This included the protection of Japan, the Philippines, and Australia and New Zealand, all of which were regarded as essential parts of free-world strength in the Pacific. The United States was also willing to consider the possibility of including Indonesia as a way of completing the offshore island chain.

But this pattern raised some touchy problems. If the Philippines were the only one of the Southeast Asian countries to be included, this would have a bad effect on the other countries in that area which were left out. It would also look like an invitation to the Communists to extend their influence over these other states, since by implication the United States was saying that it was not prepared to come to their assistance in case of attack. If the United States included Indonesia as part of the island chain, then the implication was even stronger that it was not planning to come to the aid of any country on the mainland.

But the military authorities of the United States looked askance at any arrangement which obliged it to extend its protection to all of the Southeast Asian countries. Such an arrangement might compel it to spread its strength so widely that it would have no reserves and would be vulnerable at every point. On the other hand, if the Pacific pact included only the United States, Australia, and New Zealand, it would have the appearance of a banding together of white powers as against yellow and brown.

In the end it was decided to have three interlocking pacts: first, a bilateral one between the United States and Japan which would provide for Japanese security through the presence of American troops there on the invitation of the Japanese government; second, a bilateral pact between the United States and the Philippines which would recognize existing obligations and put them on a mutual basis; and third, a three-power pact including the United States, Australia, and New Zealand which would reassure those countries of American assistance in the event of renewed aggression from Japan and thus reconcile them to a Japanese peace treaty that provided for some degree of rearmament by Japan.[3]

Dulles pushed ahead as rapidly as possible toward final drafts of the peace treaty and the security pacts. He was aware that the favorable atmosphere resulting from his trip to Japan and the South Pacific would soon begin to wear off unless very definite progress was made toward the conclusion of a settlement. He was also aware that the British Foreign Office was likewise working on a draft, and he was anxious that the American formulation should be ready first and thus should be the basic document for discussion. This might have been due to a fear that the British draft would open up some problems, such as the signing by the Chinese Communists, which would entail a considerable delay in moving toward the settlement and thus forfeit the opportunity then existing for pushing through to conclusion the kind of a treaty the United

[3] Note that the proposed security pact had "the dual purpose of assuring combined action as between the members to resist aggression from without and also to resist attack by one of the members, e.g., Japan, if Japan should again become aggressive." Note also that the United Kingdom was worried about a pact including the Philippines and possibly Indonesia, because to identify in this way the island chain would increase the danger to the mainland, particularly the United Kingdom's positions in Hong Kong and Malaya.

DIRECT NEGOTIATIONS ON THE TREATY

States wanted. Dulles' anxiety to beat the publication of the British draft was apparently not due to any pride of authorship on his part or to any plan to gain special advantage for the United States, since he was already at that time contemplating inviting the United Kingdom to act as co-sponsor with us of the treaty.

In the midst of these efforts the bombshell of MacArthur's recall was exploded by President Truman. To Dulles this act was a devastating blow, because it seemed to threaten to destroy all of his plans and earnest efforts to drive through a workable peace settlement with Japan that would change the whole atmosphere of political relations in the Far East. The General had cooperated closely with him at many stages in working out a settlement and had helped him greatly in gaining acceptance of the American position as to the proper nature of the settlement. He knew that MacArthur had great political influence in this country and the result of his dismissal might well be the disruption of the entire enterprise.

Both President Truman and Secretary of State Acheson were extremely anxious that the action taken in regard to the Supreme Commander should not halt the effort to achieve a peace settlement. The President urged Dulles very strongly to return at once to Tokyo and try to reassure the Japanese leaders that our intentions were to proceed with the negotiations without change. Dulles conferred with several Republican leaders, and, while they agreed that the action taken had greatly jeopardized the position of the peace settlement, they felt that a settlement was so vital from the standpoint of the United States in the free world that Dulles should do anything he could to help salvage the situation. He was not prepared to undertake the mission, however, unless he was satisfied that the administration was determined to proceed vigorously with the peace treaty and the security pacts along the lines already worked out and that there was no intention to change the character of the settlement—for example, by giving up the protection of the Asiatic offshore island chain.

DIRECT NEGOTIATIONS ON THE TREATY

On assurances of complete support from President Truman, Dulles agreed to go promptly to Tokyo and endeavor to reassure the Japanese officials and people that there was no change in our plans for the peace treaty.

Dulles had hoped to see General MacArthur before the latter's departure from Tokyo on April 16, 1951. However, Dulles was delayed by fog and their planes passed in the West Pacific between Wake Island and Tokyo. The following radio-telephone exchange between them as their planes passed is characteristic of the lofty language which General MacArthur could use with such skill and of which Mr. Dulles had likewise become something of a master:

MACARTHUR FROM DULLES:

I salute you. I would that we could have conferred Tokyo Sunday but fog held us at Tacoma. I stand ready to turn about to meet you Wake or Midway but understand you [are] proceeding nonstop to Honolulu.

I carry on with my mission after inner debate and consultation with and concurrence of Republican leaders who concluded we should seek to preserve the values for which we have fought, worked and prayed.

I shall adhere to our previously agreed policies. I need, want and expect your continuing counsel, guidance and support.

Ever faithfully,
April 15, 1951   John Foster Dulles

DULLES FROM MACARTHUR:

I cannot tell you how much I appreciate your fine message. You know without my saying that you can count completely upon any help or assistance I can render. Continue your magnificent work to complete a fair and just treaty at the earliest, no matter who or what may seek to obstruct you. It will be monumental in its effect and you must not fail. My best to you as always.

April 16, 1951   MacArthur

MACARTHUR FROM DULLES:

Many thanks for your uplifting message which will inspire me as I carry on.

April 16, 1951   Dulles

DIRECT NEGOTIATIONS ON THE TREATY

In his conversations with Japanese officials and in his public speeches in Tokyo, Dulles was able to reassure the people in general that the removal of General MacArthur had brought about no significant change in the attitude of the United States toward Japan and the peace settlement, or toward the Far East as a whole.

Perhaps the only noticeable change in Japan was the alteration of the public role of the Supreme Commander. The aloof and majestic style in which MacArthur had carried out his public appearances had undoubtedly served as a good psychological prop for the Japanese in the depths of their defeat. But his successor, General Matthew Ridgway, was not cast for such a role and did not try to play it. In his public appearances he did not try to dramatize his position as Supreme Commander. Instead he was open and approachable, and tended to treat the Japanese on a basis of equality. After the shock of the sudden dismissal of MacArthur had worn off, this new role of the Supreme Commander seemed to be more in keeping with the impending recovery of Japanese sovereignty.

The United Kingdom draft of the peace treaty was completed early in April 1951 and sent to the other governments of the Commonwealth. A copy was also made available to the American negotiators. It was much longer than the American version as it stood in March. The difference was largely accounted for by the greater detail on claims to property and damages. This precision was in many cases useful and, with some abridgment, the British drafting on such matters found its way into the final treaty. While Dulles had been from the start in favor of a brief and simple treaty, he had not really expected the final formulation to be as short as his original draft. He was not prepared to sacrifice agreement with the British or other Allied powers merely to achieve an esthetic triumph.

On at least one important political point, also, the British text solved a drafting problem for the United States. The American version at this stage contained nothing on the withdrawal of troops, since no way had been found to combine withdrawal of Occupation forces with the maintenance in Japan of strength enough to guarantee the country's security against Russian domination. The British draft, after stipulating that all Occupation forces of the Allied powers should be withdrawn ninety days after the treaty came into force, went on to say: "Nothing in this provision shall, however, prevent the stationing or retention of foreign armed forces in Japanese territory under or in consequence of any bilateral or multilateral agreements which have been or may be made between one or more of the Allied Powers, on the one hand, and Japan on the other." This became Article 6(a) of the final draft.

In general, however, the differences in British and American attitudes toward the settlement were still reflected in the British draft. Thus the Preamble listed China as one of the "Allied and associated powers," and Article 23 specifically referred to the Central People's Government of China. There was still a reference, again in the Preamble, to Japan's militant regime and its "share of responsibility for the war." According to Article 4 of the draft, Japan was to cede Formosa and the Pescadores to China, whereas Dulles' draft merely called for a renunciation of Japanese sovereignty in these islands. On two territorial points the British draft was harder on Japan than the corresponding American text. Japan was to renounce sovereignty in the Ryukyus, Bonins, Volcano, and Marcus Islands; and to take note of the intention of the United States to negotiate with the United Nations a trusteeship in respect of the Ryukyus and Bonins; whereas Dulles' version had merely stated that the United States might propose a trusteeship and that Japan would concur in such a proposal. In the Antarctic, Japan was to give up all future as well as present claims.

Article 9 of the British draft called for suppression of undesirable societies in Japan, and provided a long definition of "undesirable." In the next article, Japan was to undertake not to molest Japanese sympathizers with the Allied and associated powers. Neither of these provisions reached the final text. Japan was also to renounce her rights under various treaties, and to recognize the validity of the treaties of peace with Italy, Roumania, Bulgaria, Hungary, and Finland and of the prospective treaties with Austria and Germany. These latter clauses seemed unnecessary to the American negotiators; but, as there was no firm opposition, they survived.

Article 23 of the British draft earmarked Japanese gold stocks for reparations, while Article 28 transferred Japanese property in neutral and ex-enemy countries to the Allied representatives there. In Article 27, the Japanese government undertook to compensate its nationals for property taken by the Allied and associated powers in their territories. Of these three points, only the second survived American objections, and then with the qualification that the property should be handed over to the International Committee of the Red Cross for distribution to Allied prisoners of war ill-treated in Japanese prison camps. In Articles 30 and 31, Japan was to acknowledge that the war had not affected the obligation to pay prewar debts, and to affirm its liability for the external state debt. These acknowledgments became Article 18 of the eventual treaty.

Article 35 called upon Japan to negotiate a Far Eastern fisheries convention and, pending its conclusion, to prohibit Japanese nationals from fishing in conservation areas. This was an effort to satisfy Australian demands on the subject. The American draft had not limited the proposed fisheries agreements to the Far East but had spoken of "high seas fisheries," and had omitted any prohibition in the interim. Here the American draft prevailed, as far as the text was concerned, though Japan was required to give informal assurances to the Allies along the lines contemplated in the British text.

DIRECT NEGOTIATIONS ON THE TREATY

There was some feeling that the British had resorted to delaying tactics in connection with American proposals regarding the security pact and other questions, but this might readily have been explained by the fact that Mr. Bevin, the Foreign Secretary, was ill for a long period. There was also undoubtedly some concern in Britain over the actions of General MacArthur in connection with the Korean War. It was likewise quite possible that the United Kingdom was holding out on several points more on behalf of other members of the Commonwealth than on its own. Its attitude at times suggested that its resistance was designed to prevent an impression that it was not serious enough about Commonwealth interests.

It was hoped in Washington that the dismissal of MacArthur would lessen some of the irritation in Britain and other countries regarding the conduct of the Korean War. At the same time, it was important that this event should not be taken as an indication of a softening of our policy toward Communist China. Hence the British feeler as to the possibility of giving the Peiping regime in China a chance to participate in the Japanese peace settlement was quickly rejected. And so was the suggestion that Formosa be returned to "China" rather than to the "Republic of China" as provided in the Cairo Agreement. The British government was somewhat disappointed at this action but went along with the United States viewpoint.

Dulles' hint of a treaty draft sponsored by both governments was well received in London and a British working party came to the United States to help in bringing the American and British drafts together. This involved only the technical details of the settlement and not any basic policy decisions. The joint text was ready by May 3, 1951. It still showed many reservations of substance, but the limited objective of the collaboration was fully realized. The laborious specifications worked out in the British Foreign Office for the disposal of

DIRECT NEGOTIATIONS ON THE TREATY

claims and rehabilitation of contracts were incorporated and found their way almost unaltered into the final text. More importance seemed to be attached to these minutiae in London than in Washington, and undoubtedly the fact that so much of the joint draft was visibly British soothed some susceptibilities and made subsequent negotiations on more substantial issues easier.

On April 18, the Tripartite Security Pact was announced. The somewhat qualified approval with which the public in the two Pacific countries greeted this result was not shared by the Australian Labour Party. Dr. Evatt complained loudly, and not without some justification, that the announcement had been timed to influence the Australian election (which was to take place on April 28) in favor of the Liberals. Mr. Spender had had the possibility of defeat much in mind during his discussions with Mr. Dulles; and one reason for delay on the part of the Labour government in Great Britain may well have been the desire to avoid giving the Australian Liberal Party this advantage. There was much anxiety among the Australian voters about the absence in the Japanese treaty drafts of any provision for post-treaty controls on rearmament and remilitarization; and if Menzies' government had not had the compensation of the security pact to offer, its position would have been most precarious. Its defeat would have been a decided embarrassment to Dulles and his colleagues in their effort to achieve a settlement that would secure Japan for the democracies.

The remaining policy questions called for discussion at the policy-making level. Dulles, who had long since become a well-seasoned air-traveler, again stepped aboard an overseas airplane, this time bound for London and Paris. The main problems still left were the question of China's participation in the settlement, the ultimate disposition of Formosa, and various questions relating to the economic and financial clauses of the draft treaty.

DIRECT NEGOTIATIONS ON THE TREATY

The question of Chinese participation proved to be the most stubborn. All of the formulas that had been tried came up against the fact that Britain had recognized the Peiping regime and the United States still dealt with the Nationalist government as the legitimate government for China. On the other side, there was strong opposition in the British Labour Party to any concession that might lead to representation of China by the Nationalist government. The United States formula left the question up to the Japanese after the peace treaty had gone into effect. But since this opened the possibility that the Chiang Kai-shek government would be chosen as representing China, the cabinet of the British Labour government rejected the formula.[4]

After some fruitless discussions Dulles left London for Paris, where he went over the whole treaty draft with Alexandre Parodi, Secretary-General of the French Ministry of Foreign Affairs. The French raised three demands: (1) that Japan should pay them two billion dollars in reparations; (2) that Japan should conclude a commercial agreement protecting French trade interests in Indochina against "dumping"; and (3) that the three associated states of Indochina—Laos, Cambodia, and Vietnam—should participate in negotiation and signing of the treaty. Dulles explained the reasons for the treaty draft provisions bearing on these points and it was agreed that further discussions would be carried on through regular diplomatic channels. The French case on the third point was eventually recognized, and the three associated states of Indochina were allowed to sign the final treaty as independent sovereign states.

Dulles returned to London and, after further discussions, an accord was finally reached on the terms of the treaty and the procedure for concluding it. Neither the Nationalist government nor the Peiping regime was mentioned by name in

[4] See *New York Times*, June 9, 1951, 3:5, dispatch by Raymond Daniell from London.

DIRECT NEGOTIATIONS ON THE TREATY

the final text of the treaty, thus presumably leaving the matter open for Japan eventually to decide. In regard to the disposition of Formosa and the Pescadores, the treaty provided merely that Japan renounced all right, title, and claim thereto. This was in accord with the United States position.

The other questions on which agreement with the British was reached were economic and financial ones. These are discussed in the next chapter.

CHAPTER VII

THE ECONOMICS OF THE SETTLEMENT

THROUGHOUT most of the discussions with the Allied powers, Dulles and his colleagues had pursued the aim of constructing the peace settlement in such a way as to make Japan a strong and loyal ally in our conflict with the Soviet Union and its friends. Scarcely a clause in the numerous successive drafts of the treaty had escaped prolonged scrutiny with a view to determining how it would be likely to influence, not only the fortunes, but also the temper of a Japan once again free, hypothetically, to choose between the democratic and totalitarian worlds. Time after time, Dulles reiterated two basic ideas— in order to win the minds and hearts of the Japanese people to the cause of the free world, Japan must be treated as a fully sovereign independent nation and dealt with on a basis of full equality; in order to keep her in the camp of the free nations, she must be permitted to establish a working economic system that would make it possible for her population to look forward to a rising standard of welfare. The economic issues, no less than the political, were profoundly affected by this basic aim and by the different ideas of various Allies as to its implications.

Many studies were made during the Occupation of trends in the Japanese economy, of ways and means to increase production and facilitate distribution of the products, and also of the conditions under which the economy might achieve self-support without benefit of trade with Communist countries. It is not clear, however, that these studies revealed any firm basis for long-term calculations as to the viability of the Japanese economy. A baffling number of variables were involved and it was extremely difficult to get any clear picture of

THE ECONOMICS OF THE SETTLEMENT

the costs of maintaining Japan as one of the free nations. The decision had to be made in part at least on the strength of an intuitive conviction that somehow the economic and other consequences could be worked out for at least a few years, and that possibly by then a different pattern for the political world would have emerged.

By the time active negotiations began for a settlement with Japan, the whole mainland of China, including Manchuria, was under the control of the Central People's Government and the Soviet Union. Thus what had been an important source of raw materials and markets for Japan would be accessible to her henceforth only on terms agreeable to one or both of the partners in communism.[1] For the purpose of prudent calculation, it had to be assumed that no country could meet those terms and remain firmly attached to the Western alliance. Moreover, trade with China would strengthen our opponents in the current conflict. Believing these things, the government of the United States not only hoped that Japan would enter into no general political or economic agreement with Communist China, but also took certain positive steps to dissuade the Japanese government from such a course. Although the proposed treaty of peace contained no prohibition against Japan's having economic or political relations with Communist China, the United States negotiators sought and obtained assurance from Prime Minister Yoshida that he and his followers had no intention of establishing relations with Peiping. While the Occupation continued, it embargoed all

[1] The proportion which trade with China bore to total Japanese trade has been exaggerated, as has also the prospect of renewed interchange if Japan entered into political and economic relations with the Central People's Government. See Jerome B. Cohen, "Economic Problems of Free Japan," Center of International Studies, Princeton University, 1952, pp. 80-84; also *idem*, "Japan's Foreign Trade Problems," *Far Eastern Survey*, xxi, No. 16 (November 19, 1952), p. 169. But the approximately 11 per cent of Japanese imports and exports for which, by Professor Cohen's own reckoning, what is now Communist China accounted before the war is obviously far from negligible.

THE ECONOMICS OF THE SETTLEMENT

but a trickle of trade with the Communists. After the end of the Occupation, the United States government used its position as a large purchaser of supplies for the war in Korea, as chief source of economic and technical aid, and as general sponsor of Japan's readmission to the company of sovereign states, to resist the demand in Japanese business circles for expanded trade with China.

The British did not have the same conviction that keeping Japan on our side meant stopping trade with Communist China. Until June 1951, they had hoped that in some way or other the Central People's Government could be associated with the peace settlement; and when they then agreed that neither Formosa nor Peiping should be invited to sign the treaty, they understood that Japan's post-treaty choice between the two claimants to Chinese sovereignty would be a free one. They seem to have hoped that Japan would eventually recognize and enter into trade relations with Communist China, and that this outlet for Japanese manufactures would relieve the pressure on markets, in South and Southeast Asia and elsewhere, upon which Britain depended for important earnings on exports. Not having the same conviction that Japan should remain free of economic ties with Communist China, they did not feel the same obligation as the United States negotiators felt to clear away other obstacles to Japanese economic recovery, still less to stimulate that recovery by positive assistance. In fact, some of them showed symptoms of doubt whether Britain would gain enough in military security from having Japan as an ally to compensate for what it would lose in dollars from having her as an unrestricted trading competitor.

On this last point Dulles showed no doubts whatever. He repeatedly pointed out that if Japan were to be drawn into the Communist orbit and its large industrial potentialities were added to the strength of Russia and China, the consequent shift in the balance of power would be disastrous for all the

THE ECONOMICS OF THE SETTLEMENT

free nations. Hence he believed that it was imperative to keep Japan as a willing ally regardless of the economic costs that were involved. It is well, however, to have some idea of the magnitude of the problems involved in placing Japan in the role of an industrially strong and rearmed partner in the current world conflict.

Before the war, the 72,000,000 people of the Japanese islands depended upon overseas sources for 20 per cent of their food and 27 per cent of the raw materials used in their industries. All the raw cotton and all the wool for their textile industry, which was their largest exporter, had to be imported. All their rubber, 90 per cent of their oil, 95 per cent of their lead, 65 per cent of their iron ore, and considerable, though lesser, percentages of their aluminum, zinc, coal, and wood pulp were brought in from overseas.[2]

These monumental deficits in resources were partially filled by Japan's colonial empire, and by Manchuria and North China, where Japan exercised *de facto* control. Thus Korea and Formosa provided a very large percentage of the food imports, while what is now Communist China supplied roughly a third of the imported raw materials. The rest were paid for by exports of raw silk and manufactured goods (especially textiles), by shipping, insurance and banking services, and the proceeds of foreign investments.

Today, Formosa and Korea have ceased to be Japanese dependencies and the quasi-colonial relationship with Manchuria and North China has been liquidated. Japan, with a population swollen to some 90,000,000 and no corresponding increase in home food production, must compete, in markets now wholly outside her control, for the food and raw materials which she cannot produce in sufficient quantity, and for the earnings to pay for them. The development of nylon has cut

[2] For a summary of the situation in the 1930's, see, e.g., Miriam S. Farley, *The Problem of Japanese Trade Expansion in the Post-War Situation*, New York, Institute of Pacific Relations, 1939, especially pp. 31-34.

THE ECONOMICS OF THE SETTLEMENT

the demand for raw silk and for silk manufactures. Surplus earnings on the ocean-carrying trade, insurance, and foreign investments were among the casualties of the war. War losses in industrial plant and merchant marine increased the difficulties of producing and marketing manufactures for export. In absolute figures production and exports have increased markedly since the war, but they still have some distance to go before they can make American aid unnecessary and bring the standard of living of a greatly increased population up to the prewar level.

Food imports cost $337,000,000 in 1950 and rose to $558,000,000 in 1951. Total imports in 1951 reached 55.5 per cent and total exports only 31.4 per cent of the 1934-1936 level, leaving a deficit on merchandise account of $689,000,000. Japan's share of world production in the same year stood at 2.3 per cent as against 4.3 per cent in 1937, despite the increase of more than 20,000,000 in population.[3]

During the Occupation the United States spent 2 billion dollars to establish and maintain a standard of living in Japan compatible with what we conceived to be our obligation as chief occupying power. From the beginning of the war in Korea, special procurements for military purposes, together with the expenditures of the United Nations forces based in Japan, enabled the country actually to add to its dollar holdings in spite of the large deficit on merchandise account. But such profitable by-products of the struggle with Soviet communism eventually dried up and it is unlikely that the American taxpayer will be willing to continue indefinitely filling the broad gap that has ensued between the return on exports of goods and services and the cost of necessary imports. Of course the rehabilitation of Korea called for large amounts of goods and services from Japan. But this provided only temporary relief.

Short of drastic changes in economic policy, nothing like

[3] Cohen, "Economic Problems of Free Japan," pp. 8, 18, 61.

THE ECONOMICS OF THE SETTLEMENT

the necessary expansion of outlets can be found in the United States, Britain, or continental Europe. The relevant economies are for the most part not complementary but competitive, and protect themselves stubbornly with tariff walls and other import restrictions. The chief burden of external assistance in raising the Japanese economy to a viable level falls inevitably on the United States. This country has already adjusted its tariff rates to aid Japanese trade with us, but it is doubtful how much farther we can go without meeting formidable opposition from American industrialists.

Latin America offers some promise. But the chief economic hope of the American sponsors of Japan's alliance with the Western world lies in South and Southeast Asia.[4] These regions figured prominently in Japanese prewar trade, more prominently as a source of raw materials than Manchuria and China.[5] Now their multiplying populations, newly conscious of the possibility of higher living standards and eager to break the economic shackles that still bind them to other nations, are demanding more and more of the sorts of goods that Japan can supply. The colonial powers which once used their political supremacy to reserve a large share of this market against the competition of cheaper Japanese products have either been ousted or compelled to recognize fiscal autonomy. The countries of South and Southeast Asia can supply much of the food and raw materials that Japan so desperately needs. They will not of course be content merely to move from dependence on the West to dependence on Japan. They have more fear of Japanese domination than of any renewed imperialist drive from the West.

[4] See Gordon Gray's *Report to the President on Foreign Economic Policies*, November 10, 1950, Washington, D.C., G.P.O., pp. 45-47; and Dulles' statement to the Senate Committee on Foreign Relations, January 21, 1952, in Hearings, *Japanese Peace Treaty and Other Treaties Relating to Security in the Pacific*, U.S. Senate, 82nd Congress, 2nd Session, Washington, D.C., G.P.O., 1952, p. 28.

[5] Cohen, "Japan's Foreign Trade Problems," p. 169.

THE ECONOMICS OF THE SETTLEMENT

The common ambition of these countries is to industrialize to the point of being able to supply themselves with many of the things that Japan hopes to sell them. There will be a considerable period during which they will need, in addition to Japanese consumption goods, Japanese machinery for their industrialization. After that, Japan, like other nations that must import and export to sustain their populations, will have to rely upon the hope that the spread of industrialization will mean more, not less, international exchange of goods. Meanwhile, the United States has endeavored, by assistance under the Point Four Program and by the stimulation of private investment, to accelerate production in South and Southeast Asia so that they could largely replace China and Manchuria as sources of supply for Japanese products. Needless to say, such a policy did not make friends of the British and continental European traders who also attached hopes to the markets of India and Indonesia.

Throughout the negotiation of the Japanese peace treaty, the American negotiators manifested a constant sense of responsibility for the economic future of Japan as a friend of the West while resisting every proposal which held any threat of impeding her economic recovery. At an early stage the other governments concerned, excepting always of course Moscow, accepted the principle of building up Japan as a willing friend and strong ally. But they did so with some misgivings on the economic or political side, or on both. They felt that they were taking chances in security and solvency. Having acquiesced, they knew that they must pay a share in the price of keeping Japan on our side. But how much they would be willing to pay, and how cheerfully they would pay it, was not finally determined when the question of principle was decided. That took bargaining, and the answer at each stage depended not merely upon their estimate of Japan's worth as an ally, but upon calculations of what they would gain or lose in American

THE ECONOMICS OF THE SETTLEMENT

assistance and favor by supporting or opposing terms advocated by the United States.

The British Commonwealth was in the midst of a painful readjustment of its role in the politics of the Far East. Only recently it had been the most influential Western power there and had dominated the external trade of the area. The network of British commercial houses, bankers, and shippers provided the basic structure of the commercial relations between East and West.

Now, after losing much of its colonial empire, it was trying to hold on to as much of its commercial empire as it could, and also to maintain an influential role in the politics of Asia. It still held Hong Kong and Malaya, and it counted other Asian countries as part of the sterling area.

When it came to constructing a peace settlement for Japan, the statesmen of the United Kingdom of course had to acknowledge the superior position of the United States. But they could hardly be blamed for wanting to play a role that was something other than a rubber stamp. Having for so many years been accustomed to calling the tune, they were reluctant to descend to the role of an obedient player. They had differed with the United States on several major questions—notably, that of recognition of the Peiping government. It was natural, therefore, that they should try their own hand at a draft treaty. Of course they were well aware that in the end they would have to go along with the United States wherever it had a firm policy. But they had had too long an experience in the Far East to be content to follow meekly in our path. They wanted to play an active role, and also to show the rest of the Dominions that London was still looking after their interests.

The American decision to oppose reparations was based at least as much upon direct political considerations as upon the desire to safeguard Japanese recovery. Dulles' knowledge of what had happened in the case of Germany after the First World War made him believe that no reparations worth bar-

THE ECONOMICS OF THE SETTLEMENT

gaining for could actually be collected, and that they could be a bone of contention not only between victors and vanquished but among the victors themselves. The attempted enforcement of a schedule of deliveries would keep Japan in a state of confused and resentful impoverishment, while for the Allied powers it would yield little but quarrelsome frustration. He did not succeed in winning the complete waiver of claims on reparations account; but neither the abstract principle of obligation stated in the treaty, nor the scarcely less abstract plan of industrial service by which the obligation was chiefly to be fulfilled, promised much loss to Japan or gain to the victims of her aggression.

The political profit, in terms of Japan's fidelity to the West, of what seems to have been a bearable burden of reparations can only be established with time. Meanwhile, some losses on this account have been marked up. Sharp dissatisfaction with the provisions for reparations explained the delay in ratification of the treaty by the Philippines and also figured among the reasons why Burma and Indonesia did not become parties. The economic benefits to Japan, on the other hand, scarcely admit of doubt. To have added a burden of 15 or 20 billion dollars to the difficulties facing that country would have meant condemning it to indefinite servitude.[6] The American negotiators were able to avert a number of detailed economic restrictions upon Japan, and their services in this respect, notably in

---

[6] The conclusion reached in the "Statement by U.S. Representative on FEC Concerning Japanese Reparations and Level of Industry" (press release by Department of State, May 12, 1949) had specific reference only to removals of industrial equipment on reparations account, but it accurately defines the later position of the United States on reparations in general. The pertinent passage reads as follows: "The evidence contained in these reports [Overseas Consultants and Johnson Committee, reports of March 2 and May 19, 1948, respectively], and the common knowledge of all Far Eastern Commission countries, leads to the inescapable conclusion that the Japanese economy can be made to bear additional economic burdens, beyond those directly related to meeting its own requirements, only by prolonging or increasing the staggering costs borne by the American taxpayer."

THE ECONOMICS OF THE SETTLEMENT

the matter of shipbuilding capacity, were a substantial boon to the Japanese economy. But probably nothing else that they were able to do equaled in value this liberation from the prospect of a gigantic levy on money and goods.

Great Britain, Australia, and New Zealand, long after they had relinquished any hope of substantial reparations, still demanded payment of a few small items on this account. Only gradually did the firm resistance of the United States induce them to abandon the claim that Japanese gold stocks should be divided among the victors. Our representatives had to assemble strong arguments against this. One was the unlikelihood that the victors could agree on their shares. More than two years of discussion in the Far Eastern Commission had yielded no agreement on the division of industrial equipment marked for removal as reparations.[7] Another was Japan's great need of currency reserves. Dulles and Allison were unmoved by the British argument that to keep this reserve for Japan was to put an enemy guilty of aggression in a better position than its victims. Japan must overcome obstacles enough before she reached an economic position which would enable her to make any contribution to the defense of the free world. But here, as in so many questions of dollars and cents arising in the course of the negotiations, the *coup de grace* was the insistence that, if Japan could afford to hand over such assets, the United States would have the first claim upon them in reimbursement of relief expenditures during the Occupation. Faced with the dilemma of seeing the gold either left with Japan or absorbed by the United States, our Allies finally saw no purpose in insisting upon our taking it.

The United States never attempted to get back for Japan assets which had been seized in the countries at war against her. These were destined to be the most substantial form of reparation paid by the loser. It was even agreed that obligations of Japan and Japanese nationals, if expressed in cur-

[7] See statement quoted in the previous footnote.

THE ECONOMICS OF THE SETTLEMENT

rency other than that of Japan, should be taken over on the same account. This last was a concession made by the United States government at the time of Dulles' visit to London in June 1951. It was a compromise, the British having pressed for all Japanese obligations, whether in yen or in any other currency.[8]

Japanese assets in neutral and enemy countries were another possible source of at least fractional compensation; and the British for a long time demanded that they should be appropriated on reparations account. The American negotiators placed the value of those in neutral countries at about 20 million dollars, and believed that realization would be as difficult as that of German assets in Switzerland had been. They concluded that seizure would prove an unprofitable irritant to all concerned. On the assets in countries that had been at war with the Allied powers, they reserved their position. A compromise was eventually found in the Australian suggestion that both groups of assets (or their equivalent if Japan so wished) should constitute a fund out of which some compensation could be paid to Allied prisoners of war who had suffered undue hardships in Japanese camps. This became Article 16 of the treaty.

Thus the original intention, set forth in the Far Eastern Commission's Basic Post-Surrender Policy of June 19, 1947, to exact "equitable reparation of the damage caused . . . to the Allied powers" had shrunk to a small percentage. What happened to the accompanying intention to eliminate industries which would enable Japan to rearm?

The abandonment of this stipulated condition of peace was the bitterest pill that Australia and New Zealand had to swallow in the entire transaction. Their sharp distaste was shared by those countries of South and Southeast Asia which had suffered under Japanese occupation. The countries of the British Commonwealth, meeting at Canberra in August and

[8] See Article 14 (a) (2) (II) (v) of the Treaty of Peace with Japan.

THE ECONOMICS OF THE SETTLEMENT

September 1947, had repudiated any notion of using the treaty as a mode of warding off Japanese economic competition. "Any restrictions imposed on the Japanese economy," said their final communiqué, "should not go beyond what is demanded by considerations of military security." But "it was felt that key war industries such as armament and aircraft manufacture and the production of strategic materials of an uneconomic character should be prohibited. Production and capacity in key industries which could form part of war potential should be limited to defined levels. These restrictions in the interest of security should be supplemented by control of Japanese imports."

These restrictive ideas were still strongly represented in the deliberations of the Working Party which, under instructions from the Colombo Conference, met in London in May 1950. Delegations from Australia, New Zealand, and South Africa still held that machinery should be established in Japan to control, among other things, the output of industries that might contribute to rearmament. They quickly learned, however, that the British government, following the United States, had by this time abandoned the notion of direct controls in Japan, and they fell back upon a vague proposal to achieve the same results by a long-range screening of exports to that country. They were still refusing to face squarely the fact that the United States policy-makers had veered entirely away from forced disarmament of Japan and would soon be actively encouraging a measured rearmament there.

The abandonment of controls and the encouragement of rearmament were entirely logical sequels of the decision to win over Japan as an ally. Even if one believed in the efficacy of foreign controls—and Dulles, who never forgot Germany under the Versailles Treaty, did not—one could not make a friend of a country by indefinitely repressing the wide variety of industries whose products might assist in rearmament. And, if one wanted an effective partner for defense, the sooner he could begin to accumulate arms and men trained in their use, the better. Certainly there would always be some risk that he might turn his attacks against one. But Dulles did not consider this risk to be grave. He believed that Japan was already persuaded that her interests lay on the anti-Communist side, and that this persuasion would become firm conviction under the influence of Allied generosity.

Nor was it enough that Japan should be supplied with such arms as the Allies, more especially the United States, might be willing to provide. The United States would not undertake to pay indefinitely for the country's military equipment. Dulles' aim was a nation willing and able to bear the main burden of its own defense. Only such a nation would have the morale that could be depended upon in an emergency.

Australia and New Zealand never ceased protesting this feature of the treaty. As Mr. Casey, the Australian Minister of External Affairs, stated in Parliament, they gave up the struggle for restrictions on rearmament only when they found themselves in a hopeless minority opposed to the principal Allies.[9] When they finally acquiesced, they did so as part of the price that they must pay for the Tripartite Security Pact, and in further consideration of the fact that the retention of American forces in and about Japan under the Japanese-American Security Pact would itself tend to prevent a resumption of aggressive designs.

Once the principle has been acquiesced in, however grudgingly, that rearmament within limits was to be encouraged, the proposals to control the output of industries that might contribute to rearmament, whether by machinery established in Japan or by the external screening of Japanese imports, fell to the ground. All that remains is the clause in the Preamble to the Japanese-American Security Pact, where Japan's anticipated assumption of increasing responsibility for her own de-

[9] See Commonwealth of Australia, *Parliamentary Debates*, Wednesday, February 6, to Thursday, February 21, 1952, pp. 20-21.

THE ECONOMICS OF THE SETTLEMENT

fense is qualified by the proviso, "always avoiding any armament which could be an offensive threat or serve other than to promote peace and security in accordance with the purposes and principles of the United Nations Charter." How such a distinction is to be made or enforced is left unspecified. Again, however, the United States seems to have assumed a large moral responsibility, this time to the Allies who are counting upon us to check any resurgence of aggressive military power in Japan.

It was relatively easy for the American representatives to take a position opposing restrictions that would impede Japan's economic adjustment to the new conditions facing her. The standard of living in the United States did not depend to nearly the same extent as that of its Allies on exports. As for imports, those from Japan had dropped from 8.7 per cent of our total intake in 1931-1935 to 1.9 per cent in 1951.[10] The Japanese would want, of course, to increase this percentage; and much larger American purchases of their goods might well prove indispensable to Japan's prosperity. There were or would be energetic protests, accompanied by demands for increased tariffs, from tuna fishermen on the Pacific coast, and from the manufacturers of sewing machines, toys, glassware, and china in various parts of the country. But it was unlikely that any probable flow of Japanese goods in the next few years could be regarded as a serious menace to large-scale American interests. The anxiety of shipping concerns on the score of a rebuilt Japanese merchant marine represented something more substantial. But, weighed against the cost of continued direct aid, or against the probable increase in defense outlay if Japan were driven by economic stringency into alliance with the USSR and Communist China, this interest also shrank into a distinctly minor category.

The American negotiators well knew that the liberties which

[10] See Cohen, "Economic Problems of Free Japan," pp. 67-68.

THE ECONOMICS OF THE SETTLEMENT

they were so strenuously seeking for Japan might eventually have formidable consequences. Every important decision involves risks. Their calculations in the economic sphere did not pretend to embrace all the eventualities of an indefinite future. Such calculations as they made offered the hope of conciliating, in greater measure than the discarded alternatives of restriction and control, all those interests of the United States and of the free world in general which they believed to be involved in the existing situation. Given the basic logic of the settlement, their position seemed to be one of the necessary bricks in the foundation for that settlement.

Their judgments on the relative values involved, and the choices which followed from them, were ratified by American opinion, even in representative commercial and industrial circles. As early as April 1951, the National Association of Manufacturers had come out in favor of relaxing trade controls and making Japanese industry self-supporting.[11] The Board of Directors of the United States Chamber of Commerce declared its approval of the treaty.[12] So did the Thirteenth National Convention of the C.I.O.,[13] and the Executive Council of the A.F. of L.[14] Taking a point of view which seemed to be nation-wide, these bodies were not thrown off balance by the grievances of particular industries.

In the matter of Japanese shipbuilding capacity, the government of the United States took a stand which was opposed not only by a number of our Allies but also by important organizations at home. Great Britain, supported by Australia and New Zealand, continued for a long time to urge the "lopping off" of what they regarded as the excess wartime development in this part of Japan's industrial structure. Here expansion had gone beyond the needs of a peaceful Japanese

[11] *New York Times,* April 15, 1951, 46:8.
[12] *Business Action,* November 24, 1951.
[13] This took place during the week ending November 26, 1951.
[14] *Washington Post,* February 3, 1952.

THE ECONOMICS OF THE SETTLEMENT

economy to meet the needs of a great wartime navy. The Australians and New Zealanders were chiefly concerned with the implications of this development in terms of potential naval power; while for the United Kingdom this aspect of the matter, though important, was probably less disturbing than the threat to the British ocean-carrying trade. In the early days of the Occupation, excess shipyards had been earmarked for removal as reparations. Later, when this form of compensation was stopped on the initiative of the United States, the argument took the form that the plant, material, and finance absorbed by this inflated industry should be shifted to the production of consumption goods needed in Japan. It was thought that the resulting reduction in the import surplus would substantially improve the country's balance-of-payments position.

Shipping interests in the United States took the same stand, and were reinforced by the American Legion and the Veterans of Foreign Wars.[15] They did not prevail over the government's conviction that, in the current world shipping shortage, Japan would need all her existing resources to repair the ravages of war on her merchant marine sufficiently to meet her post-treaty transportation requirements. If she got to the point of making a net profit in the carrying trade, this would help to meet deficits on merchandise accounts.

It could hardly have been foreseen that general rearmament in response to the Russian threat would so tax all the industrial resources of the Allies that Japan would find it highly profitable to build ships on foreign order, in spite of the fact that the difficulty of procuring the necessary raw materials put her prices far above those of British shipbuilders. There is no reason to believe, however, that foreknowledge of this development would have altered the decision. The American negotiators would probably have seen no adequate reason why Japanese shipbuilders should not be in a position to compete with those of other countries. True, the argument that

[15] *New York Journal of Commerce,* March 1, 1951.

THE ECONOMICS OF THE SETTLEMENT

their entire capacity would be needed to meet Japan's own shipping requirements would have been put out of court; but the contribution to a needy economy by shipbuilding to foreign order would have taken its place.

As late as March 1951, the British government was still urging that Japanese shipbuilding capacity above an agreed tonnage should be destroyed. But the British draft of the treaty, communicated to the State Department in April 1951, omitted any such provision. This concession does not appear to have been made in consideration of any specific *quid pro quo*. It was probably intended to allay the restiveness on the American side over what was regarded as a somewhat niggardly response of Britain to America's willingness to compromise. On the major issues, London and Washington were in harmony. Even in some matters of detail the British government was proving obdurate less on its own account than as spokesman for other members of the Commonwealth. The United States had conceded a number of political points, as when it agreed that Japan should not be obliged to apply for membership in the United Nations or the Allied powers to support an application it made, and when it accepted the demand that Japan should surrender any existing (although not future) claims in Antarctica. It had even weakened on an economic issue when it consented to requiring 100 per cent compensation for damage to Allied property in Japan. It did not hesitate to remind the United Kingdom that compromise must be a two-way street. His Majesty's government, having reached the conclusion that Washington was unlikely to yield, and desiring, for reasons of prestige among others, to act as a co-sponsor of the joint draft, helped to smooth the common course by ditching the proposal to curtail a competitive branch of Japanese industry.

Two British proposals of a restrictive nature caused some perplexity in the American camp. One had to do with Japan's

THE ECONOMICS OF THE SETTLEMENT

renunciation of her rights under the Congo Basin Treaties of 1919, the other with her withdrawal from the Board of Directors of the Bank for International Settlements. The Congo Basin Treaties, by stipulating equality of treatment for the commerce of all nations, had made it possible for Japan to capture the Congo market for cheap textiles. The United Kingdom wanted a revision that would deprive Japan of what practically amounted to a monopoly. Revision would be possible only with the consent of all the parties. Japan was a party and could be expected in the normal course of events to veto such a change.

It was not immediately clear to our representatives how the removal of Japan as a party to these agreements would benefit British trade. The freedom guaranteed was not limited to the parties. The Americans nevertheless resisted what was merely the first step toward a revision as one of a group of stipulations that would in one way or another impede Japanese recovery. In this case the British persisted. They anticipated opposition in Parliament, especially from representatives of Lancashire spinning and weaving constituencies, to a treaty which would do so little to prevent fresh inroads upon British markets. It was important for the government to demonstrate its concern for the fortunes of a great exporting industry.

By the middle of May 1951, the United States was prepared to agree that Japan should be treated like Italy in regard to the Congo treaties. Article 42 of the Treaty of Peace with Italy reads as follows: "Italy shall accept and recognize any arrangements which may be made by the Allied and Associated Powers concerned for the modification of the Congo Basin Treaties with a view to bringing them into accord with the Charter of the United Nations." In the June 1 draft the United States was still adhering to this position, which of course did not meet the British specifications. But by June 14, after Dulles' visit to London, the British draft had been accepted. The text

THE ECONOMICS OF THE SETTLEMENT

of that date is on this point identical with the treaty.[16] Thus what seemed to be a very minor deprivation for Japan was acquiesced in by our negotiators as an incident to the compromise of the larger issues being negotiated at that time.

When the treaty eventually came before the House of Commons for approval, the British stand on the Congo Basin Treaties found some justification. Japan's renunciation of her rights was expounded with appreciation by the Member for Rochdale, third largest cotton-spinning center in the United Kingdom, who voted for ratification. The East African market apparently meant a great deal to his constituents, and while it is not suggested that this sop was the main factor influencing the Honorable Member's vote, the fact that he could hold out to his constituents some prospect of positive action in their behalf was obviously helpful to him. His motives were probably the same as those of the vast majority of the House, and it would be an injustice not to mention this feature of the debate. Mingled with sympathy with those who felt themselves threatened by a renewal of Japan's ruinous prewar competition was a general conviction that to use the treaty of peace as a means of throttling the recovery of Japanese industry and commerce would be incompatible with the generosity of the settlement and injurious to the prestige of Britain. Other means must be found, some of them within the trades concerned, to meet the main forces of the anticipated attack on British markets.[17]

Equally puzzling was Britain's insistence on ending Japan's right to share in the administration of the Bank for International Settlements. This relic of the attempt to solve the transfer problem in German reparations after the First World War was now proving a useful and modestly profitable clearing

---

[16] See Article 8 (b). The Conventions of St. Germain-en-Laye therein mentioned are more commonly known as the "Congo Basin Treaties."

[17] See *Parliamentary Debates*, House of Commons, Monday, November 26, 1951, pp. 936-38, 1005. The vote was 382 for and 33 against the treaty.

THE ECONOMICS OF THE SETTLEMENT

agency for European central banks and for the European Payments Union. Its business was wholly European, and the British proposal probably had no other motive than to bring the institution under exclusively Western control. Japanese financial houses owned 19,770 of its 200,000 shares. These were worth about 7 million dollars at current quotations, and there was no question of expropriating them, though it was intended that they should be purchased by other existing shareholders.

This was a small item in Japan's financial position, but again the United States opposed its surrender, primarily on the general principle of fighting all paring of Japanese resources, but perhaps also from doubt whether an apparently trifling proposal might not cover something more important. However, by May 1951, our negotiators were ready to agree that Japan should renounce her position as a Director of the Bank for International Settlements, subject to the express proviso that the disposal of the Japanese-held shares should be a matter for private arrangement. In the June 1, 1951, draft of the treaty it was stipulated that the surrender should not include the shares. This stipulation was omitted from the June 14 draft and from the final text of the treaty, presumably because (since they did not belong to Japan but to Japanese financial institutions) the shares would not be affected unless explicitly mentioned.

Of greater importance was the debate over the treatment to be accorded to the commerce, property, and persons of citizens of the Allied Powers. In harmony with its general policy of non-discrimination in trade, the government of the United States wished to impose upon Japan the obligation to grant most-favored-nation or national treatment to the interests of Allied nationals. But, in line with its desire to see the country restored as rapidly as possible to a position of equality, it was determined that this obligation should apply only in relation to countries granting similar treatment to Japanese interests. The United States grants most-favored-nation treatment to Japanese trade and has made strenuous efforts to persuade other countries to do the same.

Our allies had been far from willing to bind themselves not to discriminate against Japanese trade. They feared a resumption of "dumping," and of trade practices, such as concealment of the origin of goods, which had helped to make Japanese competition so formidable before the war. If these tactics were again resorted to, they wished to be at liberty to impose discriminatory restrictions on Japanese goods. France at one time proposed that, for an initial period after the treaty, Japan should be bound to grant most-favored-nation treatment without any condition of reciprocity. Britain insisted on retaining freedom of retaliation.

The treaty as finally drafted leaves the Allies free to treat Japanese commerce as they choose. However, if they discriminate against it, they cannot demand most-favored-nation or national treatment in respect of the same method. Japan, on the other hand, is bound to grant such treatment to Allied nationals in every matter in which the Allied power grants it. The initiative thus rests in the hands of each of the Allies.[18] France was not content with this outcome, and as late as July 1951 was suggesting that all mention of most-favored-nation treatment be omitted. Her protests were not strong enough to move the American negotiators, and she conceded the point.

As we have seen, Britain had pressed for the elimination of what she considered excess Japanese shipbuilding capacity. She also proposed that, as part of the national treatment stipulated in the treaty, Allied shipping should be admitted to the Japanese coastal trade. This would have had the double advantage, from her point of view, of reducing Japan's need for new ships and providing more business for British shipping. The United States successfully resisted this invasion of a domain customarily reserved to nationals, and by Article 12(d)

[18] Article 12.

Japan was permitted to refuse the privilege. She might also make exceptions to most-favored-nation or national treatment if they became necessary to safeguard her external financial position, her balance of payments, or her essential security interests. But—and here the special British preoccupation with shipping won a point—exceptions designed to safeguard her financial position or balance of payments might not be made in respect of shipping or navigation. Unless an Allied power was discriminating against Japanese shipping or her essential security interests were at stake, Japan must grant the shipping of that power national treatment.[19]

In the later years of the Occupation, SCAP devoted a great deal of effort to the expansion of Japanese trade outlets. Trade and payments agreements were made with more than thirty countries. But the fear of renewed Japanese competition continued to be strong in several important countries. Some that were willing to trade on most-favored-nation terms, so long as the American Occupation authorities were there to complain to in the event of unfair practices, were loath to commit themselves for a future in which Japan would be once again independent. In Australia, Britain, France, and to a lesser extent in the United States, manufacturers were crying calamity over the premonitory signs of a flooding of markets with the products of cheap Japanese labor. These products, it was emphasized, were often superficially indistinguishable from home manufactures, and the purchaser would have to look hard to find any indication of foreign origin. There were complaints of unlicensed use of patents. On some items the prices were only a small fraction of that asked for goods of the same type made at home.

In the circumstances, it would not have been surprising to witness a determined drive for treaty clauses that would impose levels of wages and conditions of labor in Japan, together with a code of international commercial ethics. No such drive

[19] Article 12(d).

THE ECONOMICS OF THE SETTLEMENT

developed. It early became evident that the United States would not participate in a system of controls adequate to enforce such conditions and rules on Japan. The countries concerned were forced to rely chiefly upon the growth of trade unions in Japan to bring about the wage increases and improvements in working conditions that would narrow the wide gap in costs between their products and those of Japan.

As for unfair international trading practices, by May 1950 the British Commonwealth Working Party was considering the suggestion that a voluntary declaration by Japan would probably be as effective a safeguard as could be hoped for. In the end, this is the way in which the problem was handled. The Preamble to the Treaty serves as a vehicle for the statement of Japan's intentions in the field of labor conditions and commercial ethics. These include promotion of human rights in accordance with the Universal Declaration; the effort to achieve "higher standards of living, full employment, and conditions of economic and social progress and development," as laid down in Article 55 of the United Nations Charter; and finally, the observance "in public and private trade and commerce" of "internationally accepted fair practices." Clearly a Japan keeping faith in respect of these declarations will be doing everything possible to meet any reasonable complaint on the part of commercial competitors. In this context, as in so many others, she has been formally restored to the position of a respected equal in the company of states.

Another difficult question related to fisheries. For some time before the war, the operations of long-range Japanese fishing vessels, described as floating canneries, were a cause of anxious concern to fishing interests on the Pacific coast of the United States. The energetic activities of these craft and their fleets of boats in regard to the salmon fisheries in Bristol Bay were especially resented. The salmon there were regarded by American fishermen as property of the United States. They were believed to be in danger of extermination if the Japanese

THE ECONOMICS OF THE SETTLEMENT

were allowed to fish at will. In 1938, the Japanese government agreed to prohibit its nationals from taking salmon in Bristol Bay, pending a final settlement with the United States on the control of North Pacific fisheries. Japanese fishermen did continue, however, to fish for crab in those waters, and their operations farther south along the coast of Canada and the United States were still regarded with jealous anxiety by the fishing industries in both countries. The halibut and sockeye salmon fisheries, protected by American-Canadian treaties, were thought to be endangered by foreign operators not bound by the treaties and the legislation implementing them.

In Australia the invasion of the pearl fisheries around the northern coasts and the activities of Japanese fishermen in New Guinea waters had evoked repeated protests from the local interests. Southern Korea, the Philippines, and Indonesia shared the widespread anxiety that an essential source of food would be depleted by the far-ranging and ably organized operations of Japanese fishing fleets.[20]

Fish provides almost 90 per cent of the animal protein consumed by the Japanese people. The fishing fleets were once again not only supplying this large and essential part of the nation's food, but bringing in the raw material for exports of fish products. The annual catch, 8.6 billion pounds in 1951, was about double that of the United States, which ranks as the next greatest fishing nation. Eighty-five per cent of the catch was taken in Japanese coastal waters; but for the remaining 15 per cent Japanese fishermen scoured the Pacific and Indian oceans. Unlike the merchant marine, fishing fleet tonnage had more than doubled—from 526,000 gross tons in 1934-1939 to 1,200,000 gross tons in 1951.[21] Before the war, the activities of this energetic industry were resented not only

[20] Both the Netherlands and Indonesia singled out the fisheries article of the treaty (Article 9) as one which they would have desired to amend. See "Japanese Peace Conference, Record of Proceedings," Department of State Publication 4392, December 1951, pp. 197 and 222-23.
[21] See Cohen, "Economic Problems of Free Japan," p. 15.

as a threat to the fishing interests of the riparian states, but as a possible cover for espionage, smuggling, and illegal immigration. Some charges to the same effect were again being voiced.

There were unofficial suggestions that Japanese fishermen should be confined to home and neighboring waters;[22] but no such proposal was pushed by any of the Allied Powers. To have put an article to this effect into the treaty would have been a conspicuous violation of the accepted principle of treating the defeated enemy as an equal. It would have also constituted an impediment to Japan's economic recovery. With the prospect of an increasing population in a reduced territory, Japan would be forced to rely more than ever upon the products of the sea for her food supply. There was, however, too much agitation in the United States as well as in several other Allied countries to permit Japan complete liberty of expansion in this field. The case for some restriction was strengthened by the development, since before the war, of national and international conservation schemes which operated far beyond the limits of territorial waters. These schemes limited the fishing rights of the participants, and if other nations could come into the conservation areas and fish at will, the whole purpose of the schemes would be defeated. The dilemma faced by the negotiators was how to meet the reasonable demands of Japan, now being cultivated as an ally, and at the same time to assuage the highly articulate anxieties of fishing interests in the victorious countries and prevent the frustration of laborious and costly measures of conservation.

The United States, which was in this context no less interested than its Allies, held that the matter was one with which Japan must be permitted to deal as a sovereign state. This meant that the most that could be done in a treaty of peace

[22] See DSB, xxvi, No. 662 (March 3, 1952), p. 341.

THE ECONOMICS OF THE SETTLEMENT

would be to bind her to negotiate agreements on the regulation and conservation of fisheries with such Allies as desired them.

At one stage the Canadian government was concerned about the absence of any time limit for the commencement or ending of negotiations of such agreements; but this was brushed off as contrary to the principle of sovereign equality. More serious was the demand from other members of the British Commonwealth, as well as from Canada and from the Netherlands, that the obligation to negotiate be coupled with a Japanese undertaking to prohibit fishing in conserved areas, pending the conclusion of agreements. This would put a heavy premium upon promptitude, and upon readiness to accept terms suggested by the Allied countries concerned. From the United States side it was pointed out, moreover, that "conserved area" might cover anything from an arbitrary declaration by one state to an exclusive arrangement between two or more. Any of the Allied Powers might hold up negotiations indefinitely, enjoying meanwhile the benefits of a "provisional" prohibition.

Finally, all the parties, some of them a little ruefully, accepted a voluntary statement by the Japanese government, in this instance entirely outside of the treaty. In February 1951, during his visit to Japan, Dulles had received a letter (in good State Department style) from Yoshida stating his government's intention to prohibit Japanese resident nationals and vessels from fishing in conserved fisheries where they were not conducting operations in 1940. Specifically mentioned as subject to this protection were the salmon, halibut, herring, sardine, and tuna fisheries in the Eastern Pacific and Bering Sea. On July 13, 1951, at the prompting of the United States, the Japanese cabinet made a public announcement that this intention extended to conserved areas anywhere. The prohibition was to be enforced by a commission representing both government and industry in Japan, and observers appointed by interested foreign governments were to be admitted to sit with it.[23]

Quite apart from the presumed good faith of the Japanese government, there will probably be enough Allied influence in Japan for some years to insure the working of this voluntary undertaking. The limitation to fisheries in which the Japanese were not operating in 1940 may restrict the usefulness of the arrangement to some of the countries concerned, for, except in relation to the United States and Canada, this leaves nothing in the bond to prevent immediate resumption of activities in progress before the war. The American and Canadian interests are protected by the specific enumerations of fisheries in the Eastern Pacific and Bering Sea.

Article 9 of the treaty merely requires Japan to "enter promptly into negotiations with the Allied Powers so desiring for the conclusion of bilateral and multilateral agreements providing for the regulation or limitation of fishing and the conservation and development of fisheries on the high seas." The first countries to negotiate with Japan were the United States and Canada. By December 14, 1951, a conference of these three countries held in Tokyo had produced a draft convention. This provided for a North Pacific Fisheries Commission, in which the three nations would participate and which would have power to study and recommend from time to time new conservation measures or the relaxation of existing measures. Where a stock of fish was being fully utilized by one or two of the parties under conditions necessary for maintaining maximum sustained productivity, the other party or parties would agree to abstain from fishing. Thus Japan would abstain from fishing halibut off the coasts of Canada and the United States, while Canada and Japan would abstain from

[23] DSB, xxiv, No. 608 (February 26, 1951), p. 351. In order to benefit from the prohibition, the Australian government introduced in Parliament, simultaneously with the bill to approve the treaty, legislation to conserve maritime fisheries. Commonwealth of Australia, *Parliamentary Debates*, Wednesday, February 6, to Thursday, February 21, 1952, p. 22.

THE ECONOMICS OF THE SETTLEMENT

fishing salmon in the eastern part of the Bering Sea.[24] Japan also would be entitled, under the conditions laid down in the draft, to define fisheries from which the other parties would then be required to abstain.

The economic features of the Japanese peace settlement may be summed up as follows: Japan suffers economically as well as politically in the loss of her colonial and quasi-colonial territories. The harsh and flimsy structure of her "Co-prosperity Sphere" has come crashing to the ground. She must find new markets and sources of supply to replace those from which she is shut off in East Asia. She has lost overseas assets. She has undertaken to make token reparation for her aggressions in the form of manufacturing and technical services, if any Allied power whose territory was occupied and damaged demands such services in conformity with Article 14 of the treaty. But she has not been left subject to monetary tribute. Her merchant fleet has not been taken from her. Her shipbuilding capacity has been left intact and is busily engaged in building on foreign account. The early postwar policy of earmarking for removal as reparations plant then considered surplus to a peaceful economy was prevented, largely by disagreement among the Allied Powers, from substantially reducing Japan's machinery of production. There is nothing in the treaty or in its accompanying declarations and understandings to prevent Japanese industrialists, traders, and ocean carriers from becoming once again formidable rivals of their counterparts in the Allied countries. The greatest of Japan's conquerors is systematically assisting her toward a stable and prosperous economy. Her potential value as an ally against expanding Soviet communism has spared the nation some of the deprivations, as well as humiliations, which commonly follow abject defeat in a great and prolonged war.

[24] See text in DSB, xxvi, No. 662 (March 3, 1952), pp. 342-46.

CHAPTER VIII

THE SAN FRANCISCO CONFERENCE OF 1951

THE ACCEPTED procedure for concluding a peace treaty after a coalition war has been to hold a full-dress peace conference, at which the terms of peace are agreed upon by the victors and presented to the losers. This is obviously a sensible way to get through the complex business of restoring a status of peace, providing there is a common ground of agreement to start with among the principal participants. The assumption is that the issues have been clarified in the heat of battle and that the primary purpose is to set up the conditions under which peaceful international relations are again possible. But actually the record of coalition peace-making has been an unhappy one and the peace settlements concluded in this fashion have not been noted for their durability.

It seems to have been generally taken for granted that there would be a peace conference of the customary sort to conclude a peace settlement with Japan. The only question had been in regard to the appropriate procedure for drawing up the terms of the proposed treaty for consideration by the general conference. As we have already seen, the Soviet Union had maintained since early in 1947 that the appropriate body to perform this preparatory work was the Council of Foreign Ministers, where each party had a full veto power, but by 1950 it was already becoming apparent that the basic split between the Soviet Union and the United States in regard to the future role of Japan was irreparable. The United States accordingly opposed the demand of the Soviets that the matter be referred to the Council of Foreign Ministers.

Another obstacle dealt with above was the Soviet position that the provision against any separate peace in the United

THE SAN FRANCISCO CONFERENCE OF 1951

Nations Declaration of January 1, 1942, barred the conclusion of a peace settlement with Japan not participated in by all nations which took an active part in the war. The United States had argued that the real purpose of this provision had been to make sure that all nations at war with Japan would continue to fight until victory had been won and that purpose had now been accomplished. It denied that a single country could thereafter use this provision to block any kind of a peace treaty other than the one it desired. But the truth of the matter was that so long as the Great Powers were divided and Japan was strategically important in any conflict of power in the Pacific, there was no likelihood that a peace treaty for Japan satisfactory to both sides could be negotiated.

Dulles evaded this obstacle by giving up any idea of using the conference method for negotiating the terms of the treaty. Instead, he resorted to the procedure of negotiation on a bilateral basis through diplomatic channels. This method proved as successful as it was expeditious. As we have seen, the negotiations began in September 1950 and continued almost until the time of the San Francisco Conference a year later.

This enterprise had been spoken of by Dulles as an "eleven-months peace conference." In the long course of the proceedings, he and his associates gave to the representatives of all the other countries involved full opportunity to state their respective points of view. To meet these positions, various changes were made in the terms of the draft treaty.

It must be conceded that, under the circumstances, the choice of this procedure was a good one. There was no doubt but that the Kremlin was prepared to use every possible device to keep Japan out of the camp of the Western nations. Yet, within a relatively short time, the American negotiators were able to work out a treaty draft that was reasonably satisfactory to most of the non-Communist states, and to do it without seeming to deny Russia the opportunity to participate in the process.

THE SAN FRANCISCO CONFERENCE OF 1951

Of course negotiating on a bilateral basis is quite a different thing from negotiating in a multilateral conference. In a conference, an individual state might well draw a lot of support for a point which, in bilateral negotiations, it might not have known it could have gathered. Thus, on the ticklish subject of reparations, the United States negotiators very probably had an easier time in making their views prevail by talking to each country separately than if they had had to face them altogether in a general conference. In a bilateral negotiation, the United States representative started with a good deal of advantage on his side. But on the whole it is difficult to see how a peace treaty could have been achieved by any other procedure.

The long and arduous business of negotiating the terms of the treaty was now nearing its end. In the course of the proceedings, Dulles had flown over a hundred thousand miles and his associate, John M. Allison, had likewise covered exhausting distances. It seems that only in an air age could this unique type of peace-making, involving so many different countries around the globe, have been at all feasible.

Dulles often expressed in public the belief that policy choices made in accordance with moral law are also the most practicable in the end. There are of course many who are not so sure that virtuous behavior is always rewarded with material success in this world, and they even question whether the linking of the two in the making of a choice of action does not somehow taint the moral impulse. But there are no grounds for saying that Dulles would have chosen a less virtuous course if the practical gains from such a course had been more promising. One can only be glad that in this case the magnanimous policy was also the one that offered the best chances of material benefits.

The final draft was virtually ready in July 1951, and the problem then was to get the treaty concluded and signed by the largest possible number of states without seeming to de-

THE SAN FRANCISCO CONFERENCE OF 1951

prive the Soviet Union or any other state an opportunity to express its views, but at the same time to prevent the Communist bloc from obstructing the adoption of the settlement.

It would have been possible to have signed a series of identical bilateral treaties and thus avoid a general conference altogether. But a number of the Allied Powers had expressed the desire to have an opportunity, prior to the actual signing, to make statements regarding the treaty and their aspirations for peace.[1] It was also believed that the reentry of Japan into the international community would be given far greater significance if it were marked by an impressive public ceremony in which a large number of states recorded their agreement.

Dulles' decision that the United Kingdom should be invited to join in sponsoring the treaty was also a wise one. As we have seen, there had been many differences of view between the American and British negotiators on the terms of the draft, and the British had yielded to American arguments at many points. By having them join with the United States in sponsoring the treaty, it was possible to draw them into the active support of the settlement at the Conference.

The main problem, of course, was how to arrange a conference that would include Communist nations as participants but would not be subject to being blocked by them. If discussion of any provision of the proposed treaty and possible amendment were allowed, the Soviet Union would be in a position to reopen the whole negotiations and to cause an indefinite delay. Therefore the proceedings had to be designed in such a way as to prevent any reconsideration of the text of the treaty, while at the same time permitting the participants to make statements of their views on the settlement.

The Conference opened at the Opera House in San Fran-

[1] See remarks by Dean Acheson at the First Plenary Session, in *Conference for the Conclusion and Signature of the Treaty of Peace with Japan, San Francisco, Calif., September 4-8, 1951, Record of Proceedings*, Department of State Publication 4392, Washington, D.C., G.P.O., 1951, p. 37.

THE SAN FRANCISCO CONFERENCE OF 1951

cisco on September 4, 1951, and after the customary welcoming ceremonies quickly resolved itself into a battle between the Soviet bloc, which was determined to block the adoption of the treaty, and the Allied Powers, who were endeavoring to get the treaty signed without any modification. This contest greatly enlivened the proceedings of a conference that might otherwise have been submerged in a sea of oratory. The last-minute decision of the Soviet government to be represented at the Conference aroused great public interest in the proceedings and gave the Conference more news value than it otherwise would have had. The Soviet Union sent a large delegation headed by one of their most skillful conference performers, Andrei Gromyko. They were backed up by delegations from Poland and Czechoslovakia.

The moves to keep the Soviet delegation from wrecking the Conference were primarily in the hands of Secretary of State Dean Acheson as chief delegate of the United States, and Mr. Dulles, the second member of the delegation. Acheson, who presided at the opening sessions as temporary President and later as President of the Conference, let it be known from the start that he would "conduct these proceedings in such a way as to realize the purpose for which the Conference was called"[2]—that is to say, to achieve the signing of the treaty without the reconsideration of any of its terms.

The opening strategy of the sponsors of the treaty was to get a set of rules of procedure adopted immediately which limited the agenda of the Conference to the specific actions outlined in the oral statement made to the participants at the time the invitations were issued. This agenda allowed no room for discussing any possible modification of the treaty.

After the motion to adopt the rules of procedure had been made and seconded, Gromyko endeavored to raise a prior question in regard to the composition of the Conference. He proposed that the government of the Chinese People's Repub-

[2] *Ibid.*, p. 38.

THE SAN FRANCISCO CONFERENCE OF 1951

lic be invited to send a delegation. He argued that this question should be acted upon first before considering the rules of procedure, since all those who were to participate in the Conference should do so from the very beginning.

It was obvious that if the question of inviting the Chinese Communist regime to participate was not dealt with before the rules of procedure were adopted, it would be very difficult to get it on the agenda afterward. But it was also obvious that if the question raised by Gromyko was thrown open for discussion, it might well cause a long delay in the proceedings. Acheson ruled that the Soviet motion was out of order,[3] on the ground that a prior motion had already been made and seconded. After a vigorous discussion, Gromyko appealed from the ruling of the Chair. After a further sharp interchange, this time involving the delegate from Poland, Stefan Wierblowski, the question of sustaining the ruling of the Chair was put to vote and was approved by a vote of 35 for and 3 against. Fourteen states did not vote.

The Polish delegate then proposed that the rules of procedure should first be discussed thoroughly before being acted upon, and that a committee should be appointed to study them as well as any other drafts submitted by other delegations. This was again clearly intended to delay the Conference, and was again ruled out of order. Later on, Gromyko again brought up the question of representation of Communist China but Acheson ruled that, under the rules of procedure just adopted, the proposal of the Soviet delegate was out of order. Article 7 of the rules provided that "Representation at the Conference shall be confined to the plenipotentiary delegations accredited respectively by the Governments of the Allied Powers invited by the Government of the United States of America to participate in the Conference."

Gromyko asserted that these two rulings cut off the proposal of the Soviet delegation without discussion. At first they had

[3] *Ibid.*, p. 40.

THE SAN FRANCISCO CONFERENCE OF 1951

been told that the proposal was out of order because of the prior motion to adopt the rules of procedure; then they were told that, the rules having been adopted, their proposal was out of order thereunder. However, as Acheson pointed out, the delegate of the Soviet Union could get a vote of the Conference upon his proposal by challenging the ruling of the Chair. This was done and a vote was taken on the ruling of Mr. Acheson. The vote sustained the ruling by 46 to 2. On demand of the delegate of the Soviet Union, the vote was counted again in order to record the number of those who had consciously abstained. This time the vote was 36 in favor of sustaining the action of the Chair, 3 opposed, and 2 abstentions.[4] This still left ten member states which did not wish to be recorded in any of these categories.

In regard to the question whether the treaty terms should be discussed, the Communist representatives resorted to a number of different attempts to reopen the negotiations, but these were all defeated. In the course of the heated debate, Russia was put in the peculiar position of vigorously defending the right of all states, big and small, to have a voice in the proceedings. As pointed out by the delegate from Ceylon, this was a strange position in view of Russia's past insistence that the drafting of a treaty should be left entirely to the four powers represented on the Council of Foreign Ministers—the United States, the Soviet Union, China, and Great Britain. In any case, once the rules of procedure had been adopted, the door was effectively closed to any debate about the terms of the treaty.

In the course of the proceedings, the Communist delegates charged the sponsors of the treaty, the United States and Britain, with dictatorial action. They argued that, since the United States had determined what countries should be invited to the Conference, it could keep out by its own decision the Communist regime in China, although that regime claimed

[4] *Ibid.*, p. 71.

THE SAN FRANCISCO CONFERENCE OF 1951

a vital interest in the proceedings. Since the rules of procedure had been drawn up by the United States and Britain, they had been free to fix the agenda in such a way as to prevent any discussion of the treaty terms. But the vigorous arguments of the Communist delegates drew practically no support from the other delegations. It was obvious to everybody that the major purpose of the Russians and the satellite countries was to delay the proceedings indefinitely and to block the settlement altogether if that were possible. The tactics of the Communists, which were a repetition of their action in other conferences, merely tended to exasperate the other delegations at San Francisco and to make them more favorably inclined toward the settlement worked out by the United States. The management of the proceedings by Acheson was extraordinarily skillful and circumspect. The Communists, on the other hand, not only were ill-tempered, but at various times seemed confused. In any case, they did not make the most of their opportunities and were beaten on every move.

It had been anticipated that the strategy of the Soviet delegation would be to try to turn the meeting into a traditional peace conference in which all the terms of the settlement were examined, and then to talk the treaty to death. This could be done on the plea that all participants had a right to be heard, and that the United States strategy was designed to block any debate. The Russian strategy failed because most delegates knew that the Russians were not seeking debate in good faith or trying to arrive at a general settlement beneficial to all. While some of the Allied Powers were still dissatisfied with some terms of the settlement, they realized that this was probably the best treaty that could be achieved under the circumstances, and that it was far better than no treaty at all. By the end of the first plenary session, it was quite clear that the Communist strategy was defeated and that the American strategy had won the day.

Most of the remaining sessions of the Conference were given

THE SAN FRANCISCO CONFERENCE OF 1951

over to statements of the views of the various governments regarding the settlement. The fact that these could have no influence in changing the terms of the treaty did not mean that they were unimportant. The Conference provided an excellent arena for elucidating the terms of the settlement and revealing the extent of the unity, or lack of it, that existed among the non-Communist states as to the future of Japan and the security of the Pacific. According to the plan adopted, the delegates of the United States and the United Kingdom first made statements presenting the treaty to the members of the Conference, and this was followed by the comments of the other delegations.

On the question of the initiative assumed by the United States in the drafting of the treaty, Dulles pointed out that at the time of victory the Allies had unanimously given to the United States the exclusive power to name the Supreme Commander and to direct the Occupation to prepare Japan for return to the status of peace. This put the United States in a position to judge when the Japanese were prepared for peace and obligated it to take timely steps to bring the Occupation to an end in due course. Dulles described the first steps toward arranging a conference to consider plans for a Japanese peace treaty and the blocking of that effort by the Soviet Union. This led the United States policy-makers to abandon the conference method, "which afforded excessive possibilities of obstruction, and to seek peace through diplomatic processes which no single nation could thwart."[5] This, according to Dulles, had been done with the hearty cooperation of most of the Allies and had resulted in a finished text.

There is no absolute value in universality over particularity in arriving at decisions. In a world of independent states, the method of unanimity has obvious advantages where the participating states are using it honestly. But so long as states remain independent, the problem of the veto is always present.

[5] *Ibid.*, p. 75.

THE SAN FRANCISCO CONFERENCE OF 1951

In the absence of a common purpose or set of values in a particular situation, increasing the number of participants in a conference tends to increase the number of those who will raise obstacles and perhaps will have to be bought off.

Even if the Communist states had not been included, it still seems quite probable that the use of the conference method in the present case would have reduced the chances of getting a magnanimous treaty. In the beginning of the negotiations, perhaps the majority of the Allied nations were less disposed to be generous toward the Japanese than was the United States. Many of them demanded controls or restrictions of one kind or another in the settlement. Had it been possible for them to present these demands on the floor of a conference, it seems probable that the United States might have been forced to yield at least to some of them. Hence it might well be argued that, even among the non-Communist states, the special circumstances indicated that a better settlement would accrue from a series of bilateral diplomatic negotiations than from an attempt to hold a general conference. However, it is not necessary to answer this question finally, since the presence of the Russians rendered it extremely unlikely that anything of value could come out of a resort to the conference method.

The fact that the diplomatic method was substituted for the conference method did not mean that the United States imposed or even tried to impose its own views about the settlement on each country in turn. According to Dulles, every nation which took a constructive interest in the treaty could claim authorship of important parts of the present text. Each of them voluntarily subordinated some special interests in order to achieve a broad base of unity. In substantiation of this, Dulles produced a comparative study of the March 1951 draft of the treaty and the August 13, 1951, text which was finally circulated. These indicated that no article of the earlier draft escaped some modification in the later one and in many instances the changes were important. Dulles further claimed that the procedure was participated in by so many nations "as to make this treaty the most broadly based peace treaty in all history."[6]

In discussing the principal provisions of the text, Dulles frequently resorted to generalizations about political behavior in justifying the steps taken or the decisions made. Thus, in explaining why certain obligations were put in the Preamble rather than in the form of legal obligations, Dulles asserted that unless the Japanese people wanted to carry out these aspirations, efforts at legal compulsion would do no good. Thus, he said, "Japan, when it applies for membership in the United Nations, should do so because it *wants* to be a member, not because the Allies compelled it. Eighty million people cannot be compelled from without to respect the human rights and fundamental freedoms of their fellows."[7]

In seeking to answer the question whether a growing population of over 80 million could survive on the Japanese home islands, Dulles recalled that when Japan had had a vast colonial empire into which the Japanese people could freely emigrate, only a few did so. He concluded that the Japanese, like other people, prefer to live at home. Even if they had more territory, they would not emigrate to it. It might be questioned whether this is an ample basis for Dulles' conclusion. One would have to go farther and seek to discover the conditions under which people were inclined or disinclined to emigrate. What is interesting to note is the frequency with which the subject of political and moral behavior crops up in the policy decisions that were made. Thus, in summing up his case, he rests it on such generalizations as the following:

> Above all, Japan needs the will to live at peace with others as good neighbors.
> All of this is possible, if we make peace now. It becomes impossible, or at best improbable, if Japan's long deferred hopes are now blasted.

[6] *Ibid.*, p. 76. [7] *Ibid.*, p. 77.

THE SAN FRANCISCO CONFERENCE OF 1951

There are, in Japan, new-born institutions of freedom. But they will not flourish if military rule continues indefinitely to be supreme.

Dignity cannot be developed by those who are subjected to alien control, however benign.

Self-respect is not felt by those who have no rights of their own in the world, who live on charity and who trade on sufferance.

Regard for justice rarely animates those who are subjected to such grave injustice as would be the denial of present peace.

Fellowship is not the mood of peoples who are denied fellowship.[8]

When the time came for the Soviet delegate to present the attitude of his government on the treaty, he made a final and crafty attempt to break through the defenses of the sponsors of the treaty and force a debate on its terms on the floor of the Conference. Following a long and bitter attack on the treaty and its sponsors, he started to propose a number of "amendments" to the treaty. The Vice President of the Conference (P. C. Spender), who was then in the Chair, broke in to ask whether the Soviet delegate was proposing to move some amendments, but he replied that he was "making a declaration" and was defending his position. He was thereupon permitted to continue his statement of what were really amendments. These included the recognition by Japan of the full sovereignty of Communist China over Manchuria, Formosa, and various other islands off the China coast; Russia was to have full sovereignty over the southern part of Sakhalin and adjacent islands as well as over the Kurile Islands, but Japan was to get back the Ryukyus, the Bonins, and various other islands then being administered by the United States; all armed forces of the Allied Powers were to be withdrawn from Japan within ninety days of the coming into force of the treaty, and after that no foreign power should have troops or military bases on Japanese territory; Japan was to pay reparations for damages caused by her military operations, the amount and sources of payment to be considered at a confer-

[8] *Ibid.*, p. 87.

THE SAN FRANCISCO CONFERENCE OF 1951

ence participated in by the nations subjected to Japanese occupation; Japan was not to enter into any coalition or military alliance directed against any power which had participated in the war against Japan; its land, air, and naval armaments should be closely restricted to the minimum size necessary for self-defense, and so forth. A new article should be added to Chapter III as follows: "1. The Straits of La Perouse (Soya) and Nemoru, along the entire Japanese coast, as well as the Straits of Tsugaru and Tsushima shall be demilitarized. These straits shall always be open for the passage of merchant ships of all countries. 2. The straits named in paragraph 1 of this article shall be open for the passage of only such warships as belong to the Powers adjacent to the Sea of Japan."

The gist of these proposals was the removal of all influence of the United States in Japanese affairs and the elimination of any United States military power in the whole area, as well as a rigorous limitation on any Japanese rearmament. In other words, Japan was to be opened up for Communist subjugation at Russia's own convenience. The last proposal quoted above, as Dulles subsequently pointed out, would mean that only the Russian naval force based upon Vladivostok could use the Straits of La Perouse, Nemoru, Tsugaru, and Tsushima. This Russian naval force would patrol the waters in and about Japan, would cut Japan in two and divide it from Korea, so that not even a United States force could operate in the straits between Korea and Japan. "That is the kind of thing," said Mr. Dulles, "the 'jokers' that are contained in the series of proposals that are put before us, and that is the kind of thing that we have had to face for 11 months, and that is why it is not possible for us to come to any agreement with the Soviet Union despite our sincere desire to do so."[9]

No action was taken in regard to the "amendments" described by Gromyko. However, toward the close of the Conference the Soviet delegate got the floor and asked in what

[9] *Ibid.*, p. 301.

THE SAN FRANCISCO CONFERENCE OF 1951

order the Soviet amendments to the treaty would be taken up, and whether a vote was intended on these amendments and in what manner. The President of the Conference reminded Gromyko that at the time of his original statement he had been asked whether he was moving amendments to the treaty and he had answered that he was only making a statement. Therefore there was no motion or any other proposal to make amendments to the treaty before the Conference. Gromyko insisted, however, that although the amendments had been put forward only as part of the declaration of the Soviet delegation, they should be treated as amendments and should be discussed and voted on in the usual manner. There was at the time a motion before the Conference that would permit only a few more statements and then the business of the Conference was to be deemed closed except for a few routine matters. Acheson ruled that, if this resolution was adopted, the opportunity to provide amendments to the treaty was foreclosed. After some additional debate a vote was taken on the resolution, which was adopted by 41 to 1. Gromyko still persisted in his efforts to force a consideration of the amendments but was ruled out of order by Acheson. This ruling was again challenged by Gromyko, and after sharp debate was put to a vote. The Conference by 46 to 3 supported the Chair and thus foreclosed the efforts of the Soviet delegate to reopen debate on the treaty.

Thus, by the skillful handling of procedure, the sponsors of the treaty were able to get it up to the point of signature without giving the USSR an opportunity to veto its acceptance. This was accomplished, furthermore, while still allowing the delegates of the Communist states a full opportunity to state their case.

The amendments proposed by Gromyko did not have the slightest chance of acceptance and were clearly not meant seriously by him. All that he had hoped for was to open a debate on the treaty draft that would lead to a vote on it in which the

THE SAN FRANCISCO CONFERENCE OF 1951

USSR could exercise its veto. This would have blocked the signing of the treaty and would have meant the failure of the San Francisco Conference. By careful planning and alert management, the sponsors defeated this objective of the Soviet Union and brought about a notable display of unity on the part of the non-Communist states represented at the Conference. Of the 52 members of the Conference, 49 states (including Japan) signed the treaty and only the three Communist states (USSR, Poland, and Czechoslovakia) refrained from doing so.

CHAPTER IX

SECURITY IN THE PACIFIC

WE HAVE SEEN that, in the long process of arriving at a peace settlement with Japan, the basic concern of Dulles and his predecessors had shifted from the traditional business of resuming peaceful relations with a thoroughly defeated state to the far more complicated enterprise of achieving a position of security against Communist expansion in the Pacific area. In this the American planners were faced not only with the full force of the Communist revolt against the existing international order, but with two other revolutionary movements that made their task exceedingly difficult. The first was the spectacular advance in nuclear weapons, altering basically the place of force in the relations among nations. The second was the ending of the colonial era and the sudden emergence into independent statehood of a large number of nations that had formerly played little or no part in international politics. These three revolutionary movements coming together had the effect of outdating most of the traditional ways of thinking about the nature of the international system and the political relations of nations. They made the problem of achieving security and stability vastly more complex.

Reappraisals of our ways of conceiving of the international arena have been slow in developing. As we have seen above, some of our leading statesmen failed to see or to comprehend the direction of the changes that were occurring in the location of power and influence, especially in the Far East. There was little speculation as to what would take the place of Japanese military power after it had been dismantled.

One exception is found in an unpublicized report on the implications of the Chinese Communist movement, prepared by the Military Intelligence Division of the War Department. This report was dated July 5, 1945, while the war with Japan was still going on, and before the Potsdam Declaration outlining the surrender terms had been drawn up.

The conclusion of the report was that the problem of postwar peace in the Far East revolved around two major questions: (1) How could the military-political vacuum in the Far East be filled following the defeat of Japan? (2) How could the United States promote internal unity in China? This implied that the type of peace we could gain by a victory over Japan would depend quite as much on what happened in China as in Japan. The independence and territorial and administrative integrity of China had been our key policy in the Far East for many years. The threats to such integrity had come from Russia and from Japan. A rough balance between these two powers had been maintained by Great Britain and the United States. One important by-product of a defeat of Japan, said the report, would be the upsetting of this whole power situation in the Far East. With the total defeat of Japan, Russia would again emerge "as the sole military land power of any account in Asia," and she would be vastly stronger there than before. The elements of uncertainty as to Soviet Russia's intentions in China were very similar to those in regard to Eastern Europe in 1943 and 1944. The fears that Soviet Russia had intended to develop Eastern Europe as an exclusive Soviet sphere of influence had proved correct. There was justification for similar fears in regard to North China, Manchuria, and Korea. Furthermore, those who believed that the Chinese Communists were not real Communists were doomed to disillusionment. Not only were they real Communists but they were the most effectively organized group in China. The general conclusion of the report was that a strong and stable China could not exist without the natural resources of Manchuria and North China, and in order to prevent the separation of the latter from China it was essential that it should not be divided (as in Europe) into American-British and Russian zones of military operations. What the authors of this report did not foresee was that the *whole* of the mainland of China would fall eventually under the influence of Moscow.[1]

Attempts of this kind to analyze the problem of peace with Japan in the light of the changing character of the whole Far East were quite uncommon at the time. Most of the policy-makers followed the pattern exemplified in General MacArthur's March 17, 1947, statement in which the Japanese peace settlement was considered in terms of Japan's own readiness to receive back her sovereign independence.

The hope of most American policy planners had been that China might again become a strong and independent as well as a friendly state which could provide the basis for stability in the Far East. To that end the United States government had provided generous assistance and had done everything possible to build up the prestige of Nationalist China. But after VJ Day, September 2, 1945, it was concluded that the only hope for a united China was for the Nationalist government to come to terms with the Chinese Communists. To help bring this about, General Marshall was sent on his mission to China in December 1945.[2] But, as we saw above, his mission failed to achieve this goal and the Communist forces continued to gain strength in China.

The jockeying among the Great Powers to improve their respective power positions in the Far East began immediately with victory. The proposal from Stalin to have a Russian general appointed to share equally with General MacArthur the supreme occupation power in Japan was turned down flatly by the United States.

[1] This report is printed as Appendix II, Part 7A, *Hearings on the Institute of Pacific Relations before the Subcommittee to Investigate the Administration of the Internal Security Act and Other Internal Security Laws*, Committee on the Judiciary, U.S. Senate, 82nd Congress, 2nd Session, Washington, D.C., G.P.O., 1952. See especially pp. 2309-10.

[2] Dulles suggests (*War or Peace*, p. 226) that the period immediately after the surrender of Japan was a time—perhaps the only time—when China might have been saved from falling to the Communist forces. But it does not appear that the government policy-makers believed this was possible.

SECURITY IN THE PACIFIC

Large and virtuous promises of good behavior by governments in general pronouncements often cause embarrassment in specific circumstances. "No territorial aggrandizement," set forth in the Atlantic Charter, was a sincerely held aim of the United States for the peace settlement. However cruel the war had been, the American leaders had no desire for outright annexation of territory which had been a part of the Japanese homeland before the war. Nevertheless, the military authorities determined that, in order to avoid another costly island-hopping war in the future, it was essential to build a powerful American base on Okinawa and to keep the former Japanese mandated islands in the Pacific from falling into the hands of a potential enemy.

Okinawa, which was a part of the Ryukyus, represented something of a problem since it was inhabited by Japanese subjects and had been regarded as part of Japanese territory for some years. The United States evaded the "no territorial aggrandizement" pledge in this case by recognizing that Japan had a "residual sovereignty" over the island, which would become full-fledged sovereignty whenever the United States ceased to need it as a military base.

The other islands in the Pacific in which the United States expressed an interest were the Marshalls, the Carolines, and the Marianas. These had been held by Japan under mandate from the League of Nations. There were 98 islands altogether, with territories totaling 846 square miles and a population of 48,000 natives. The economic resources of the islands were negligible. The bitterness of the fighting from island to island during the war had led the military leaders of the United States to the conviction that we should never again have to retake these islands from any other power. We would have to be in a position to occupy them, and to build air and naval bases on them without asking anybody's permission.

To this end the United States applied to the United Nations to designate the islands as strategic territories under the man-

SECURITY IN THE PACIFIC

date of the United States, and this was done. This meant that so long as the islands remained strategically important to us, we could do what we thought necessary in regard to them. Japan had forfeited her right to them, since she had violated her mandate over them by using them for purposes of aggression. No one else laid claim to the islands. Russia could not oppose our application, since she had already taken over the Kuriles without even mentioning the word "trusteeship."

Not all military opinion thought favorably of the idea of making Japan a bulwark against the growing strength of the Communists. There was some question as to whether the cost of maintaining military forces on the Japanese islands and supporting the Japanese economy would be worth whatever strategic value might be involved. We have already mentioned that Secretary of the Army Royall was of the opinion that Japan would be valueless in the case of war with Russia. He did not know, he said, what United States troops in Japan could do in the event of the outbreak of such a war and felt it might be better to pull them out before the war started. He was not sure that it would be worth while trying to hold the Japanese mainland so long as we had Okinawa and the Philippines.[3]

General MacArthur also had something to say on the idea of Japan as a bulwark against Russia. He held that if Russia attacked Japan the United States would certainly defend her, but he did not believe that Russia would do so. In case of another war, he said, "We do not want Japan to fight." When asked about the function of Japan in the American strategy of defense, he said, "We never intended to use Japan as an ally. All we want her to do is remain neutral. We are helping her

[3] See *New York Times*, February 14, 1949, 1:5; also Chapter IV above, p. 79. These remarks of Secretary Royall caused considerable anxiety in Japan. Later he and Lt. Gen. J. Lawton Collins made public statements intended to allay Japanese fears. See *New York Times*, February 26, 1949, 1:4.

SECURITY IN THE PACIFIC

to become self-supporting because that will relieve us of the burden of supplying her." General MacArthur was reported as being confident that Anglo-Saxon interests in the Pacific were entirely secure despite the recent Communist victories in China, and he was not worried about Communist gains in the recent Japanese elections. He said he did not think Japanese Communists had a direct link with Moscow.[4]

Along the same line of neutralization for Japan, a proposal was made for a three-power military guarantee of Japan under which the United States, the United Kingdom, and the Soviet Union would each agree to come to the aid of Japan if attacked, and to respect Japanese neutrality in any other conflict in which any one of them was involved. It was believed that neutralization of Japan was perhaps the only means of insuring Japanese security on which the United States and the USSR might agree, and that it would be better than no agreement at all. Such a proposal, it was said, would not interfere with the building up of United States strength in the Ryukyus and other outlying areas. At the same time, a serious question existed as to whether Russia could be counted on to observe any such arrangement.

Undoubtedly, the most important single event that was forcing the top statesmen to rethink their basic premises was the fall of China to the Communists. While this was scarcely mentioned in the public discussions regarding the Japanese peace settlement, it nevertheless brought a large element of uncertainty into the whole problem of security in the Pacific. In 1947 and 1948, there had been a tendency among the top officials to underestimate the gravity of the threat in China. To some extent, even Secretary Acheson seems to have done so, at least in the early days. This is suggested by his statement before a Congressional Committee on March 20, 1947, when he was testifying on the Greek-Turkish Aid Program as Acting Secretary. He then said: "The Chinese government is not in the

[4] *Ibid.*, March 2, 1949, 22:2, dispatch by G. Ward Price from Tokyo.

position at the present time that the Greek government is in. It is not approaching collapse; it is not threatened by defeat by the Communists."[5]

Secretary Acheson's remark in February 1949 that it would be better to wait for the dust to settle before making a new Asian policy was an indication of the fact that the traditional guides to action in this part of the world were no longer giving persuasive answers. Early in 1949 the Truman administration had decided not to embark on a huge program of support for Chiang Kai-shek. Beyond that it was not easy to see the proper lines of any future policy. By June it had been decided to try to halt any further extension of Communist domination on the continent of Asia or in the Southeast Asia area.[6] Ambassador Jessup conducted investigations both in this country and in the Far East, and the celebrated White Paper on China was issued in August 1949. The new policy of the United States toward Communist China was indicated by Acheson as follows: "We continue to believe that, however tragic may be the immediate future of China and however ruthlessly a major portion of this great people may be exploited by a party in the interest of a foreign imperialism, ultimately the profound civilization and the democratic individualism of China will reassert themselves and she will throw off the foreign yoke. I consider that we should encourage all developments in China which now and in the future will work toward this end."[7] But, in any case, he

[5] *Hearings on the Military Situation in the Far East*, Committee on Armed Services and Committee on Foreign Relations, U.S. Senate, 82nd Congress, 1st Session, June 4, 1951, p. 2198; quoted in *The Pattern of Responsibility*, ed. by McGeorge Bundy, Boston, Houghton Mifflin, 1952, p. 176.

[6] See instruction from Secretary Acheson to Ambassador Philip C. Jessup, July 18, 1949: "You will please take as your assumption that it is a fundamental decision of American policy that the United States does not intend to permit further extension of Communist domination on the continent of Asia or in the Southeast Asia area." (Quoted in *ibid.*, p. 180.)

[7] Letter of transmittal, *United States Relations with China*, pp. xvi, xvii.

SECURITY IN THE PACIFIC

believed that the United States must not undertake to interfere in Chinese affairs.

The customary tone of liberalism continued to run through the recurring American attitudes toward China. Secretary Acheson in his speech before the National Press Club in Washington on January 12, 1950, again recalled that for fifty years it had been the fundamental belief of the American people that the control of China by a foreign power was contrary to American interests. In this the interests of America and of China were parallel. What bothered us most in what was happening in China was not the spread of Communist doctrine so much as the attitude of the Soviet Union in using communism as a means of seizing parts of China. As Acheson stated, "This fact that the Soviet Union is taking the four northern provinces of China is the single most significant, most important fact, in the relations of any foreign power with Asia." He added that "We must take the position we have always taken—that anyone who violates the integrity of China is the enemy of China and is acting contrary to our own interests."

It was in this same speech that Acheson described our policy regarding the military security of the Pacific area. The first step was the task of assuming a military defense of Japan so long as that was required. The defensive perimeter ran along the Aleutians to Japan and then to the Ryukyus. We would continue to hold our important defense position in the Ryukyus. From the Ryukyus the defensive perimeter ran to the Philippine Islands. We would continue to carry out our defensive arrangements with them.

So far as the military security of other areas in the Pacific was concerned, it was clear, said Acheson, that no person could guarantee these areas against military attack. If such an attack occurred, the initial reliance for resistance must be on the people attacked and then upon the commitments of the entire civilized world under the Charter of the United Nations.

SECURITY IN THE PACIFIC

Elsewhere in Southeast Asia, the limits of what we could do were to help where we were wanted. In Acheson's mind, "There is a new day which has dawned in Asia. It is a day in which the Asian peoples are on their own, and know it, and intend to continue on their own. Whether the new day is bright or dark is a decision that lies within the countries of Asia. It is not a decision which a friend or even an enemy from the outside can decide for them." As we have indicated, security before World War II had been generally thought of in terms of a specific line of defense. The British land and naval forces covered South Asia down to Singapore, with its strong naval force. After the defeat of Japan the American island chain ran from the Aleutian Islands down to Manila. In the eyes of the Australians there was a dangerous gap between Singapore and Manila through which Communist forces might expand.

As a matter of fact, although Singapore remained a British naval base, there was little strength behind it to back it up. With India, Ceylon, Burma, and Vietnam more or less independent, the Empire line of defense was a weak reed to lean on as security against expansion to the south by the Chinese Communists.

The northern island chain made a little more sense, since it was generally believed that the United States would feel its own security directly threatened by any attack on the chain and would resort to substantial retaliation to protect it. However, there was some doubt as to whether the United States would do so below the Philippines and there was still a gap to the south around which an aggressor might move. If we wished to believe in the idea of a defense line in the Pacific, we would have to convince the Sino-Soviet bloc that we were prepared to deter effectively any move of the Communists anywhere down to Australia.

SECURITY IN THE PACIFIC

When Dulles went on his negotiating visit to the Pacific in January and February 1951, he bore with him authority to explore the possibilities of a security pact embracing Japan, the Philippines, Australia, New Zealand, and possibly Indonesia. He was not to consider the inclusion of Malaya, Indochina, or Hong Kong, for the Pentagon was at this time opposed to any commitment to military action on the mainland of Asia. The threat to Europe was demanding more of our rare divisions, we were already dangerously engaged in Korea, our mobilization was only just getting under way, and, in general, the military preference was for obligations that could be fulfilled principally by naval and air forces, without calling for any extensive use of land units.

On his way, Dulles learned that Indonesia, while it would probably like to be invited, would almost certainly refuse to join in any arrangement which would openly commit the government to the Western democratic side in the current world conflict. It had recognized the Central People's Government in Peiping, it was fighting communism at home, it was under strong nationalist pressure to keep clear of any new Western imperialism, and it desperately needed a period of peace in which to attack a bewildering accumulation of urgent internal problems. Taking its cue from India, it was therefore proclaiming its intentions of following its own line of policy, veering neither to the Soviet nor to the democratic bloc. Its subsequent brief digression to sign the treaty of peace with Japan was corrected by refusal to ratify that instrument, and by rejection of any compromising military aid from the United States.

Doubts about a part for Indonesia in a Pacific security pact, already entertained in Washington before Dulles' departure, were thus confirmed; and our envoy by-passed the struggling new republic without profound regrets. He had other obstacles, more threatening to any meaningful Pacific pact, to cope with. Perhaps the main purpose in mind was to compensate Australia and New Zealand for Japanese rearmament; but these countries would have nothing to do with a treaty which would oblige them to come to the defense of the late and still feared aggressor. If they must forgo controls in Japan, what they wanted as a minimum was firm assurance from the United States that they would be defended against any new threat from that quarter. Moreover, they had another reason for not committing themselves to defend Japan. That was their obligation to assist Great Britain in the Middle East. Their fear of overextending themselves also militated against guaranteeing the Philippines; but on this they would have been willing to stretch a point, provided always that the United Kingdom would agree.

We have already discussed in Chapter VI the negotiation of the ANZUS Pact. The British government would have welcomed a pact that would include Great Britain and cover Malaya and Hong Kong. Since this was not available, it objected to an arrangement which would exclude Great Britain but include the two Pacific Dominions. And it objected most strenuously to an arrangement which, while excluding the United Kingdom, would impose on Australia and New Zealand the obligation to go to the defense of the Philippines. The British government, after all, considered itself bound to defend the two Dominions if they got into trouble. In vain Dulles argued that the inclusion of the Philippines would remove the taint of a Western device designed to perpetuate foreign domination in the Orient. The British insisted that the special relations existing between the United States and a former possession would merely aggravate such suspicions.

After long delays and much argument, the suggestion made originally in Canberra was adopted. The United States offered a separate, bilateral mutual defense treaty to the Philippines, and this was accepted. A bilateral security treaty had already been worked out with Japan. The security structure surrounding the treaty of peace with Japan would thus consist of bilateral arrangements made with Japan and with the Philippines, and a tripartite arrangement with Australia and New Zealand. The scheme as a whole received a tepid blessing from the United Kingdom, whose original reluctance was increased by the refusal of the Council set up under the tripartite arrangement to admit any United Kingdom representation.

The three treaties were consistently described by the Democratic and Republican administrations in this country as mere stopgaps, pending the conclusion of a regional security system for the Pacific. As Secretary of State, Dulles almost immediately set about the task of discovering under what conditions the existing patchwork could be consolidated and extended into a unified structure for the whole Pacific and Far Eastern area.

There were influential voices urging decisive American leadership in this direction. From the specific instances of the Organization of American States and NATO, Governor Dewey leaped to the following generalization: "The outstanding fact is that, wherever we have undertaken treaties assuring collective action in advance, there is no war. Peace has thus far been preserved by strength. In the Pacific we have done only patchwork jobs and that area is racked by five wars. . . . I am confident that the Chinese will not attack if the United States develops, within the structure of the United Nations, a total Pacific treaty of mutual defense."[8]

For this idea Dewey found enthusiastic support in President Quirino of the Philippines. The conflicts of interest which defeated Quirino's own attempts to bring his neighbors together into a defensive alliance left New York's governor undaunted. He disposed of regional jealousies and the yearnings for a comfortable neutrality with such glowing brush strokes as this: "Perhaps Indonesia and Burma might

[8] Thomas E. Dewey, *Journey to the Far Pacific*, Garden City, N.Y., Doubleday, 1952, p. 334.

drag their heels for a while but I am confident they would join in the end. Then, though India and Pakistan, not being Pacific nations, were not members of the alliance, they would have time to work out their complicated problems without being surrounded and choked to death before they get on their feet."[9] Mr. Dewey's geography, it will be noticed, was as supple as his optimism.

In addition to the three security treaties mentioned above, a treaty of mutual defense was signed by the United States and the Republic of Korea on October 1, 1953.

These commitments were brought together, after a fashion, by the Southeast Asia Collective Defense Treaty (SEATO), which was signed at Manila on September 8, 1954. Later a Mutual Defense Treaty between the United States and Formosa was signed on December 1, 1954, and this was accompanied by an undertaking by the Nationalists not to attack the mainland of China without the consent of the United States.

The obligations of SEATO, like those of ANZUS, were by no means as broad as those of NATO. The member states merely agreed that, in the event of armed aggression against one of them, or against any state or territories unanimously designated, they would act to meet the common danger "in accordance with their constitutional processes." There was no definite commitment to military assistance in specific circumstances. Dulles had made it clear that there was no possibility of getting the NATO type of commitment through the Senate of the United States. Furthermore, the United States had added a stipulation that it was only concerned with "Communist aggression," and not with aggression in general.

SEATO did, however, provide for mutual cooperation to deal with subversion in addition to armed aggression, and thus opened the door slightly to the possibility of legalized intervention in internal affairs.

[9] *Ibid.*, pp. 166-67.

SECURITY IN THE PACIFIC

The signatories of SEATO were the United States, Great Britain, France, Australia, New Zealand, the Philippines, Pakistan, and Thailand. By unanimous agreement Cambodia, Laos, and South Vietnam were covered by the arrangement, although they were not signatories of the treaty. At the same time the parties to the treaty signed the Pacific Charter, promising "to promote self-government and to secure the independence of all countries whose peoples desire it and are able to undertake its responsibilities."[10]

Dulles' conception at this time of the politics of the Far East and the policy we ought to pursue was set forth in a speech he made on December 4, 1958, before the California Chamber of Commerce in San Francisco. His basic assumption was that the leaders of international communism regarded the United States as "the hardest nut for them to crack," and that they hoped to do so by first getting control of as many as possible of the other nations of the world, leaving the United States so encircled and isolated that it would recognize that continuing struggle was hopeless and would "voluntarily" accept Communist domination. If that was really the strategy of the Communist leaders, then the United States had no alternative but to try to check Communist expansion in the Far East as well as in Europe.

To this end the United States had entered into the various collective defense agreements described above and, in addition, had arranged for the establishment of various air and naval bases in the Pacific region. The locations of these bases were roughly fixed by the necessary refueling distance for our manned bombers for loaded missions over the Communist area and return. Later on it was planned to use a few of these bases as launching sites for our intermediate-range ballistic missiles as they were developed.

Even after the intercontinental missiles were perfected,

[10] Pacific Charter, in *United States Treaties and Other International Agreements, 1955*, VI, Part 1, Washington, D.C., G.P.O., 1956, p. 91.

SECURITY IN THE PACIFIC

there was still some reason for maintaining the forward military bases. In the first place it was not anticipated that all use of force between the Western states and the Communists would be reduced to exchanges of intercontinental missiles. It was clear from the Russian viewpoint that they envisaged various types of conflicts between the blocs which would not justify the use of this type of warfare. As for the United States, we wanted the freedom of choice which the possession of foreign bases gave us as to the kind of a war we would fight. Such bases were intended to make up for the far greater supply of manpower available to the Sino-Soviet bloc.

In the second place, it was thought that the system of alliances and foreign bases which had been developed under our leadership would in itself be, for most purposes, sufficient to discourage the Communist states from embarking on further expansionist adventures. The bases would also give some assurance to the local populations that, in case they were attacked, we would intervene to protect them.

It is of course true that our bases abroad are at the same time within close bombing range of launching sites on Communist territory. Assuming that Communist China eventually possesses missiles and delivery systems, our bases in Okinawa and the Philippines, for example, would be within easy target distance for them. But the Communists often appear as anxious as we are to keep conflicts between us within limits and to avoid all-out thermonuclear war. They are well aware that a missile attack by them on our foreign bases such as Okinawa would doubtless trigger off a full-scale combat between us. In spite of Khrushchev's bold talk about the ease with which the Communists could demolish our foreign bases, no real move has been made against them beyond blackmail attempts aimed at the host countries. It would seem to be a fair guess that our foreign bases are safe from missile attack by the Communist bloc until it is ready to start a full-scale nuclear war.

SECURITY IN THE PACIFIC

Since Dulles first propounded his massive retaliation policy, it has been subjected to some criticism, not only by Communist leaders and by the governments of neutral countries, but also by defense specialists in this country. It was pointed out that, if this were really to be our policy, the Communists would be foolish to initiate an aggression anywhere and wait for us to retaliate against their principal cities. Their obvious strategy would be to strike first at our forces of deterrence and then proceed with their aggression without much fear that we would be able to stage a serious counterattack. Our only way to defeat this move would be to make our deterrent forces here and abroad fully invulnerable to attack, and that would be a long and extremely expensive process.

With the development of long-range missile weapons and the early superiority shown by the Russians in this field, the massive retaliation strategy has raised further questions.

It soon became apparent that, largely through the development of a greater missile thrust than the United States had so far been able to produce, the Russians would be able to stay well ahead of us in the missile race for at least four or five years. This would give them a greatly increased capability of rendering our deterrent forces ineffective. Assuming that the President of the United States were not killed in the first strike (a natural target for an aggressor against us), he would be aware that any decision by him to retaliate with the forces we had left would mean an immediate all-out attack on our cities as well as our military installations. The anticipated losses for us would be so great that it is hard to believe he would not find them unacceptable and refuse to retaliate.

It has also been pointed out that, although we insist that we would never make a first strike against Russia or anyone else, our massive retaliation against her in the event of an aggression by her on another nation would be precisely that. The President of the United States would have to make the decision for retaliation, and it is again difficult to believe that he would do so unless United States security were directly involved. That would not seem to be the case with regard to small Asian states covered in the SEATO Pact. Hence it is hard to see that in these cases the deterrent threat would really be credible to the Russians.

How will our security in the Pacific be affected by the relations of Japan with Soviet Russia and Communist China, neither of whom signed the peace treaty and neither of whom has been recognized by Japan?

At first our dominant concern was that Russia would be tempted to gain control over a powerless Japan. The industrial development of Japan and the technical skills of its people would have been of immense value to the Russian economy and would, as Dulles pointed out, have shifted the world balance of power in her favor. Accordingly, Dulles did everything in his power to keep Japan on the side of the Western powers. The American-Japanese Security Treaty, although addressed to the world at large, was aimed primarily at Russia.

However, in the years since the peace treaty was ratified, the fear that Russia would seek to make a satellite out of Japan has somewhat lessened. The Japanese people themselves do not seem to be greatly worried by a Russian coup. The United States has withdrawn its ground troops from the Japanese mainland, and this was greeted with general approval by the Japanese people.

Apparently the Russians have been convinced that we are prepared to fight a war to keep them out of Japan. In any case, they have not thought that what they might get out of making Japan a satellite was worth the risk of fighting us for it. This is one deterrent set up by the United States that has really seemed to work.

Another explanation is possible. Communist China has

rapidly come to the fore as the leading military power in Asia, and it is not out of the question that Peking would be uneasy if Russia should succeed in getting control over Japan. The further encirclement of Communist China even by an apparently friendly Russia would hardly be looked upon as a comforting embrace.

At the moment a more likely threat than that of Russian ambitions for loosening Japan's attachment to the Western camp comes from Communist China. Its leaders have proclaimed that they would like nothing better than to see the influence of the United States removed from Asia altogether. The culture of Communist China is closer to that of Japan than any other country. Both of them are "nations of Asia" and find something of a common bond in that fact. Apparently a majority of Japanese businessmen are anxious to resume trading with the Chinese. There is a large and growing demand for the renewal of diplomatic relations with Peking, even against the wishes of the United States. If the Socialist Party should get into power in Japan, there would undoubtedly be a political shift in the direction of friendship for the Communist Chinese and away from the Western alliance.

Up to the present time Communist China does not possess nuclear weapons and hence is far less of a threat to the security of the United States than is the Soviet Union. But when the day arrives that Communist China becomes a nuclear power, with or without the help of Moscow, then our security position in the Far East will be seriously compromised. It behooves us now to get ready for that day, and to meet it with a firm, efficient, and all-inclusive policy.

INDEX

Acheson, Secy. of State Dean, 62, 72, 77, 78, 80-81, 82, 83, 97, 135, 192-93, 193-94, 195; at peace conference, 176-79, 185

Advisory Committee on Postwar Foreign Policy (State Dept.), 6n, 15-16, 17-18, 20-21, 22-23, 31

Advisory Committee on Problems of Foreign Relations (State Dept.), 3-4, 4-5

A. F. of L., 158

Aleutian Islands, 81, 194

Allied Council for Japan, 84, 85

Allison, John M., 109, 153, 174

American Legion, 159

Antarctic, J. claims in, 119, 138, 160

ANZUS Pact, *see* security treaties

Ashida, Prime Minister Hitoshi, 73

Atlantic Charter, 7-9, 13, 20, 46, 190

Australia and New Zealand, and J. settlement, 66, 67, 81, 82, 91, 115, 117, 119, 125, 128, 154-56, 158-59, 165, 167, 170n; and China, 91, 116; fear of J. militarism, 109, 117, 125, 128, 141, 197; and J. reparations, 109, 125, 153, 154; and security treaty with US, 128-29, 130-32, 141, 197-98; and Pacific security treaty, 116-17, 133-34, 195, 196, 197, 200

Bank for International Settlements, J. withdrawal from, 161, 162-63

Basic Post-Surrender Policy for Japan, *see* Far Eastern Commission

Bevin, Foreign Secy. Ernest, 64, 82, 83, 85, 140

bipartisanship in foreign affairs, US, 95-97

Blakeslee, George H., 30

Bonin Islands, 108, 111, 112, 113, 114, 119, 138, 183

Borton, Hugh, 58

Borton group postwar planning, 57-59

Bradley, Gen. Omar, 103

British Commonwealth, views on J. settlement, 66-68, 81, 169; and J. economic competition, 67, 81, 151, 154-55; Working Party proposals, 115-22; and Pacific security treaty, 116-17. *See also* Australia and New Zealand *and* Great Britain

Burma, 109, 152, 195, 198-99

Butterworth, Asst. Secy. of State W. W., Jr., 97

Byrnes, Secy. of State James F., 37n, 38, 40-41, 47, 89-90

Cairo Conference, 30; Declaration, 32, 39, 111

Canada, 110, 115, 116, 117-18, 169, 170-71

Canberra Conference (1947), 65-68, 118, 119, 120; (1949) 83, 85, 116

Carr, E. H., 10

Casey, R. G., Australian Minister of Ext. Affairs, 156

Ceylon, 101, 109, 115, 116, 118, 195

Chiang Kai-shek, 29, 30, 31, 88, 118, 142, 193

China, Communist, relations with US, 48, 50, 86, 193-94, 201; trade with Japan, 55n, 90, 94, 145-46, 145n, 149; relations with USSR, 65, 127-28, 188, 204; and conflict with US in Far East, 79, 84, 102, 124, 126-28, 133, 194-96, 201-5; "two Chinas" problem, 91, 101, 109, 113, 116, 118, 141, 143; and J. settlement, 101, 102, 112, 116, 132, 134, 140, 141-42, 157, 176-77, 178-79, 183; Military Intelligence Division report on, 187-89

China, Nationalist, relations with US, x, xi, 24, 28-29, 30, 44, 95,

205

INDEX

96, 114, 118, 188, 189, 193-94, 199; defeat by Communists, 48, 88, 95, 192-93; and J. settlement, 65, 69, 89-90, 101, 109, 114, 141-42; and J. reparations, 70, 82, 114; "two Chinas" problem, 91, 101, 109, 118, 140, 141-43. *See also* China, Communist, Formosa, *and* Manchuria
Churchill, Prime Minister Winston S., 7, 24, 25, 90
C.I.O., 158
Collins, Lt. Gen. J. Lawton, 79, 191n
Colombo Conference of Commonwealth Foreign Ministers (1950), 85, 115, 155
Colombo Plan, 132
Commonwealth Consultative Conference (London 1950), 86, 115-21, 155, 166
Communists in Japan, 60-61, 62, 76, 87, 92, 192
Congo Basin Treaties, J. rights under, 161-62
Congressional opinion, on J. settlement, 21, 62-63, 69; on postwar international organization, 26-27, 43; on China, 95
Constitution, postwar J., 54, 68n, 80; anti-war clause, 54, 56, 92, 101, 104
Containment Policy, 49-50, 60, 62, 76, 83, 95
Council of Foreign Ministers, 64, 89-90, 96, 172, 178

Davis, Norman, 19n
Declaration by United Nations (Jan. 1, 1942), 13, 46, 110, 172-73
Defense Dept., on rearming Japan, 80; on timing of treaty, 85, 105; difference of opinion with State Dept., 85, 86-88; and treaty terms, 108
Dening, Sir Esler, British Undersecy. for Far East, 82
Dewey, Gov. Thomas E., 96, 198-99

Division of Special Research (State Dept.), 5, 5n, 16, 20
Doidge, F. W., N.Z. Minister of Ext. Affairs, 125
Draper, Under Secy. William, 72-73
Dulles, John Foster, as "architect of treaty," 86; as Foreign Policy Adviser, 95-96, 97; term in Senate, 96, 98; on bipartisanship, 97, 97n; guiding principles in J. settlement, 98-102, 129-30, 144, 151-52, 155-56, 174, 181-83, 187, 200, 203; relations with MacArthur, 103, 135-36; negotiations in Japan, 103-4, 135-37; with FEC representatives, 109-10; in Philippines, 123-24; in Australia, 125-32; in London and Paris, 141-43; use of negotiation procedure, 173-74, 175, 180-81; and peace conference, 176, 180-83, 184

economic recovery of Japan, 144-71; early plans for, 40, 55, 58, 59; Allies' views on, 68, 146, 150-69; new policies of SCAP, 70-77; financial assistance by US, 73-74, 84, 129, 148-49, 156; Dulles' views on, 100, 129, 144, 146-47, 155-56; postwar situation, 147-49; and Latin America, 149; and Southeast Asia, 149-50; and US interest groups, 157-58, 159, 165, 166-67. *See also* reparations by Japan
Eden, Foreign Secy. Anthony, 8, 9, 22-23, 24, 25n, 27
Emperor Hirohito, 36, 38; retention of, 35-36, 37, 38, 40
Evatt, H. W., Australian Minister of Ext. Affairs, 67, 130, 141

Far Eastern Commission, 58, 59, 64; conference proposed by US, 58, 64-66; Basic Post-Surrender Policy for Japan (1947), 66, 67, 111, 154; measures in Japan, 71, 72, 81, 82; participation in J.

INDEX

settlement, 81, 83, 101, 107, 109-10, 116, 153; abolition proposed, 84, 85; Seven-Point Memorandum to (1950), 107-8, 109, 110, 115, 120-21
fisheries problem, 108, 119, 139, 157, 166-71
Foreign Ministers' Conference (Moscow 1943), 26, 27, 30
Formosa, 24, 25, 30, 91, 108, 111, 113-14, 119, 138, 140, 141, 143, 147, 183, 199. See also China, Nationalist
Forrestal, Secy. of Navy James, 34-35, 36, 37, 37n, 38, 56, 57
Four-Nation Declaration (1943), 25-28
France, 110, 116, 124, 142, 164, 200

Great Britain, and wartime planning, 22-25; and J. settlement, 24, 65, 82-83, 91, 121-22, 155, 160; and J. economic competition, 67, 82, 94, 110, 146, 150-51, 159-65; and J. reparations, 70, 82, 139, 153-54; recognition of Communist China, 91, 138, 140, 142, 151; and Working Party proposals, 115, 117-18, 120; and Commonwealth interests in Far East, 130-31, 134n, 140, 151, 160, 197-200; British treaty draft, 134-43. See also Australia and New Zealand and British Commonwealth
Grew, Ambassador Joseph E., 35-37, 38, 41
Gromyko, Andrei, 176, 177, 178, 182-86

Hamilton, Maxwell, 69
Harriman, W. Averell, 37
Hong Kong, 124, 134, 151, 196, 197
Hoover, Herbert, 63
Hopkins, Harry, 22, 25n, 26
Hornbeck, Stanley K., 30
Hull, Secy. of State Cordell, views on postwar planning, 3, 6-7, 8, 9-12, 13-15, 15n, 16, 17, 22-25, 32, 96; relations with State Dept., 14, 31; views on USSR, 23-24, 27-28; on China, 24, 28-29

India, and J. settlement, 82, 91, 110, 113-14, 115, 118, 132-33; and Communist China, 91, 114; role in Far East, 195, 196, 199
Indochina, 24, 101, 116, 131, 142, 200
Indonesia, and J. settlement, 101, 109, 110, 152, 167, 196; and Pacific security treaty, 131, 133, 134n, 196, 198-99
Initial Post-Surrender Policy Directive for Japan (1945), 57, 58, 66
Interdepartmental Group to Consider Postwar International Economic Problems, 5, 5n
International Court of Justice, 85, 108, 120
international rule of law, concept of, 9-12, 42, 43, 50
isolationism, US, xi, 3, 9, 12, 21, 27, 43, 95

Japan, see economic recovery, labor conditions, police force, public opinion, rearmament, reparations, shipbuilding, US-Japan security treaty, US military bases
Jessup, Philip C., 193
Johnson, Secy. of Defense Louis A., 83, 103
Johnson, Percy, 72, 73

Kennan, George F., 48, 49, 60, 74, 77, 98
Korea, xvi, 24, 30, 32, 62, 147, 148, 188; and J. settlement, 101, 108, 167; Russian proposal for, 184; US treaty, 199
Korean War, 64n, 102, 104, 128, 140, 196; effect on Japan, 73, 78, 146, 148; effect on treaty plans, 104-5

207

INDEX

Kurile Islands, 108, 111, 112, 113, 183, 191

labor conditions in Japan, 68n, 75-76, 77, 81, 165-66
Latin America and J. economy, 149
Lehman, Sen. Herbert, 97n
Litvinov, Maxim, 25
Lovett, Acting Secy. of State Robert A., 69

MacArthur, Gen. Douglas, 41, 60, 64, 68n, 78, 100, 102; views on effect of Occupation, 54, 61, 67, 89; on treaty, 54-56, 56n, 63, 103; and economic measures in Japan, 55, 72, 73-75; recall by Truman, 64n, 135-37, 140; and military measures, 79-80, 88-89, 92; relations with Dulles, 103, 135-36; views on Far Eastern conflict, 191-92
Malaya, 124, 134, 151, 196, 197
Malik, Yakov, 110
Manchuria, 24, 30, 147, 149, 150, 183, 188
mandated islands, Japanese, 24, 25n, 55, 56-57, 190-91
Mao Tse-tung, 48, 116
Marshall, Gen. George C., 34, 48, 49, 189
Menzies, Prime Minister R. G., 125, 141
Molotov, Foreign Minister Vyacheslav, 27, 28
Moscow Agreement (1945), 85, 87

National Association of Manufacturers, 158
National Security Council decision (November 1948), 77-78, 81, 83
Navy Dept., wartime planning, 19, 32, 33-35; postwar peace proposals, 56-57
Nehru, Prime Minister Jawaharlal, 132-33
Netherlands, 70, 110, 124, 169
New Zealand, *see* Australia and New Zealand

Nicolson, Harold, xiv
North Pacific Fisheries Commission, 170

Occupation of Japan, basic directive for, 33-34; shift in economic policies, 70-77
Okinawa, 37, 55, 89, 190, 191, 203. *See also* Ryukyu Islands

Pacific Charter, 200
Pakistan, 110, 115, 118, 199, 200
Parodi, Foreign Minister Alexandre, 142
Pasvolsky, Leo, 3, 5, 5n
Pauley Commission, 70, 72
peace-making process, x-xi, xii, 118, 172, 174; and wartime coalitions, xi, xvii-xviii, 172; problems of alliance formation, 51-52; conference vs. negotiation procedure, 180-81
Peace Problem Council for Japan, 93
peace treaty drafts: March 1947, 58-59; August 1947, 58-59, 70; January 1948, 58-59, 70, 78n, 102; September 1949, 78n; October 13, 1949, 80, 83-86, 98, 102; August 7, 1950, 105; British, April 1951, 134-35, 137-39, 151, 160, 161-62; joint US-British, May 3, 1951, 140-43, 160; final text, 85, 119, 134-43, 163, 164-65, 166, 170, 171, 174, 175, 182
Pescadores, 30, 108, 111, 113-14, 119, 138, 143
Philippines, and J. settlement, 82, 109, 123-24, 167; and J. reparations, 70, 82, 109-10, 123, 152; and China, 116, 203; and Pacific security treaty, 124, 133-34, 134n, 191, 195, 196-97, 198, 200; and ANZUS Pact, 131; and bilateral treaty with US, 134, 197-98
Poland, at peace conference, 176, 177, 186

INDEX

police force, Japanese, 55, 59, 77, 78, 78n, 100
Policy Committee (State Dept.), 31
policy-making, problems of, x-xi, xii-xvii, 44-45, 174, 180-81
Policy Planning Staff (State Dept.), 48, 59-62, 77, 98
Postwar Programs Committee (State Dept.), 31-32
Potsdam Conference, 37-38, 41; Proclamation (Declaration), xi, 34, 37, 39-40, 58, 67, 111, 113
Poulson, Rep. Norris, 63
public opinion in Japan, 86, 87-89, 91-94, 104, 107

Quebec Conference, 25-26
Quirino, Pres. Elpedio, 198

rearmament of Japan, 55, 56, 59, 68n, 80, 108, 111, 113, 117, 128; armament industries, 154-57
reparations by Japan, early plans for, 33, 53, 58, 59, 61, 70, 84, 171, 174; MacArthur's views on, 55; partial payments, 70; end recommended, 72; Dulles' views on, 100, 102, 123, 151-52; Allies' views on, 82, 109-10, 114, 119, 139, 142, 153-54; effect of reduction, 152-53
Reston, James, 103-4
Ridgway, Gen. Matthew, 137
Roosevelt, Pres. Franklin D., 3, 6, 13, 14, 19n, 22-23, 24-25, 25n, 30-31
Royall, Secy. of Army Kenneth C., 74, 79, 191, 191n
Ryukyu Islands, 55, 56-57, 81, 108, 111, 112, 113, 114, 119, 138, 183, 190, 192, 194

San Francisco peace conference, xii, 175-86
SEATO, *see* security treaties, Pacific
security treaties: US-Japan, 55, 61, 82, 85, 101, 102, 117, 124, 134, 156-57, 197-98, 203; US-Australia-New Zealand (ANZUS), 128-29, 130-32, 134, 141, 156, 197, 198; US-Philippines, 134, 197-98; Pacific (SEATO), 124, 133-34, 196-98, 199-200, 203
Seven-Point Memorandum, *see* Far Eastern Commission
shipbuilding, restrictions on J., 55, 153, 158-60, 164-65, 171
Singapore, 195
Soong, T. V., 28
South Africa, 115, 117, 119, 155
Southeast Asia, and J. settlement, 81; and Pacific security treaty, 133-34, 195, 196-98; and J. economy, 149-50. *See also* Burma, Ceylon, India, Indochina, Indonesia, and Malaya
South Sakhalin, 108, 111, 112, 113, 183
Soviet Union, *see* USSR
Spender, P. C., Australian Minister of Ext. Affairs, 125, 130, 141, 183
Stalin, Joseph, 8, 9, 26, 29, 30-31, 90, 189
State Dept., postwar planning, prior to US entry, 3-12; during World War II, 8, 13-21, 31-35, 42, 47; and Cold War strategy, 48-50, 89-90, 98; proposes FEC conference on treaty, 64-66, 69; difference of opinion with Defense Dept., 86-89; and USSR participation in treaty, 89, 90; and China policy, 95; Seven-Point Memorandum to FEC, 107-8. *See also* peace treaty drafts *and* security treaties
State-War-Navy Coordinating Committee (SWNCC), 33-34, 35, 57
Stimson, Secy. of War Henry L., 37, 38, 41, 57
Strike, Clifford, 73
Subcommittee on Security Problems (State Dept.), 17, 18-19, 20

Taber, Rep. John, 63
Taft, Sen. Robert A., 69

INDEX

Teheran Conference, 30, 31
Thailand, 200
trade unions, Japanese, *see* labor conditions
Truman, Pres. Harry S., 36, 37, 38, 47, 48, 49, 64n, 98, 107, 129, 135, 136, 193

unconditional surrender and Japan, 16, 19, 19n, 33, 34-35, 36, 38-39, 40
USSR, conflict with US in Far East, xii, 11, 43-44, 84, 89-90, 104, 124, 125-26, 132-33, 157, 172, 189, 191-205; question of participation in J. settlement, 6, 8-9, 58, 64-66, 69, 85-90, 92, 108-10, 116, 172-73, 178; US wartime relations with, 8, 20-21, 23-24; entry into war against Japan, 26, 29, 30-31, 34, 37-38, 39, 40; and US Cold War policy, 43-44, 48-52; and Communist China, 65, 127-28, 188, 204; as threat to Japan, 87, 93-94, 105, 106-7, 184, 203; J. settlement proposals by, 110-12, 183-84; strategy at peace conference, 175-79, 182-86
United Nations, postwar plans for, 18-19, 23; Dulles' role, 96; and J. settlement, 55, 56, 69, 93, 109, 119, 120, 166; and J. membership, 80, 101, 108, 160, 182
US-Australia-New Zealand security treaty, *see* security treaties
US Chamber of Commerce, 158
US economic assistance to Japan, *see* economic recovery of Japan
US foreign policy, wartime assumptions, 9-12, 16-17, 20-21, 32-33, 42; postwar assumptions, 42-45; formation of Cold War policy, 46-52; general objectives in Japan, 53-54, 76, 77-78; concern for security arrangements in Far East, 125-28, 133-34, 187-204. *See also* China, economic recovery of Japan, Great Britain, State Department, *and* USSR
US-Japan security treaty, *see* security treaties
US military bases in Japan, 56, 59, 78-81, 82, 87-88, 92-93, 104, 105-7, 111, 113, 114, 129-30
US-Philippines security treaty, *see* security treaties

Vandenberg, Sen. Arthur H., 96
Versailles Treaty, lessons of, 6, 15n, 17, 68, 99, 151-52, 155
Veterans of Foreign Wars, 159
Vietnam, 195
Voorhees, Under Secy. of Army Tracy, 88

Wagner, Sen. Robert, Sr., 96
Wallace, Vice-Pres. Henry A., 15
War Dept., wartime planning, 19, 32, 33-35; postwar peace proposals, 56-57; Military Intelligence Division report, 187-89
Welles, Under Secy. of State Sumner, 4, 15, 23
White Paper on China (1949), 193
Wierblowski, Stefan, 177
Wilson, Woodrow, 9, 19
Working Party, Commonwealth, *see* Commonwealth Consultative Conference

Yalta Agreement, xi, 31, 34, 111, 112-13, 113
Yoshida, Prime Minister Shigeru, 73, 91-92, 93, 104, 145, 169
Young, Ralph A., 73

Zaibatsu, SCAP policy toward, 57, 71, 74-75, 77, 81-82

Printed by Libri Plureos GmbH in Hamburg, Germany